Management
Development

Michel Syrett and Jean Lammiman

- Fast-track route to designing, delivering and facilitating management development initiatives

- Covers the key areas of how to link management development initiatives to organizational goals or strategy, conduct training needs analysis to test the real learning needs of participants, recruit and brief external experts and consultants, ensure that proper use is made of scenarios, discussions, assignments and action learning, and capture and sustain the learning that results

- Examples and lessons from some of the world's most successful businesses, including General Electric, News International, Standard Chartered Bank and Volkswagen/Skoda, and ideas from the smartest thinkers including Rosabeth Moss Kanter, Peter Senge, Chris Argyris and Reg Revans

- Includes a glossary of key concepts and a comprehensive resources guide

TRAINING & DEVELOPMENT

11.05

>> EXPRESS EXEC.COM <<
essential management thinking at your fingertips

First Published 2003 by
Capstone Publishing Limited (a Wiley company)
8 Newtec Place
Magdalen Road
Oxford OX4 1RE
United Kingdom
http://www.capstoneideas.com

CIP catalogue records for this book are available from the British Library and the US Library of Congress

ISBN 1-84112-446-X

Wiley also publishes its books in a variety of electronic formats. Some content that appears in print may not be available in electronic books.

Websites often change their contents and addresses; details of sites listed in this book were accurate at the time of writing, but may change.

Contents

Introduction to ExpressExec   v

11.05.01 Introduction   1
11.05.02 What is Management Development?   7
11.05.03 Evolution of Management Development   17
11.05.04 The E-Dimension   35
11.05.05 The Global Dimension   51
11.05.06 The State of the Art   69
11.05.07 In Practice   105
11.05.08 Key Concepts and Thinkers   121
11.05.09 Resources   133
11.05.10 Ten Steps to Making it Work   147

Frequently Asked Questions (FAQs)   155
Index   159

Introduction to ExpressExec

ExpressExec is a completely up-to-date resource of current business practice, accessible in a number of ways – anytime, anyplace, anywhere. ExpressExec combines best practice cases, key ideas, action points, glossaries, further reading, and resources.

Each module contains 10 individual titles that cover all the key aspects of global business practice. Written by leading experts in their field, the knowledge imparted provides executives with the tools and skills to increase their personal and business effectiveness, benefiting both employee and employer.

ExpressExec is available in a number of formats:

- » **Print** – 120 titles available through retailers or printed on demand using any combination of the 1200 chapters available.
- » **E-Books** – e-books can be individually downloaded from ExpressExec.com or online retailers onto PCs, handheld computers, and e-readers.
- » **Online** – http://www.expressexec.wiley.com/ provides fully searchable access to the complete ExpressExec resource via the Internet – a cost-effective online tool to increase business expertise across a whole organization.

» **ExpressExec Performance Support Solution (EEPSS)** – a software solution that integrates ExpressExec content with interactive tools to provide organizations with a complete internal management development solution.
» **ExpressExec Rights and Syndication** – ExpressExec content can be licensed for translation or display within intranets or on Internet sites.

To find out more visit www.ExpressExec.com or contact elound@wiley-capstone.co.uk.

11.05.01

Introduction

The basics of management development.

In May 1998, Marks & Spencer (M&S) was the UK's most profitable retailer. It reported profits of £2bn and its share price hit a record high of 664p per share. But in October of that year, M&S reported the first fall in profits since the start of the decade and, by the end of 1998, its share price had dropped by 32%. Two years later, the share price had fallen to less than 180p.

Bad news kept coming. Long term chairman Sir Richard Greenbury retired a year early in February 1999. His successor, Peter Salisbury, lasted only a year and a half. Perhaps the lowest point, at least in PR terms, came when 1,000 trade unionists from France, Spain and Belgium demonstrated outside the company's flagship store in London's Oxford Street over the proposed closure of stores on the continent.

Worst of all, customers were turning their backs on products offered by M&S, a firm that had once been seen as a national institution. Some commentators doubted whether the company would survive.

The turning point was the appointment of Belgian chairman Luc Vandevelde in February 2000, although the benefits in bottom line profits were not seen for a further year and a half. By that time, the company had an entirely new set of executives including managing director Roger Holmes, who came from Kingfisher.

One of the new executive team was Helena Feltham who, in July 2000, was appointed HR director. It is a sign of the importance M&S placed on the HR function that her predecessor Clara Freeman had been a main board director. Feltham inherited the status of the function but she also acquired a new and unaccustomed freedom to act.

Feltham realized very quickly that the old paternalism of the company – which provided cradle to grave security but also rigidly governed the way managers operated – was out of touch with the increasing individualism of M&S employees and society at large. The company, in her view, had lost touch with the needs of its customers because it had also lost touch with the needs of its employees.

In the late summer of 2000 she ran a two-day workshop, facilitated by London Business School's Professor Lynda Gratton, which is now seen as pivotal in the company's long road to recovery. Held at Lord's cricket ground in London and attended by 500 managers, it literally threw every tenet of management that had previously underpinned the M&S "way" into the garbage can.

Line managers were given freedoms they had never previously enjoyed. A new two-way staff communication strategy and performance management system to underpin their new style was put in place. The skills managers needed were tested using interactive "exhibits" put together by the HR leadership team which included games based on *Big Brother* and *The Weakest Link*, Punch and Judy and a basketball display. The model of management brainstormed at the workshop was later endorsed by the Board, published and sent to every employee.

It was the most successful management development event ever run by the company. One whole wall of M&S's headquarters in Baker Street was filled with congratulatory e-mails from the people who had taken part. Gratton describes it as "the most inspirational event I've been to." Many other milestones have marked M&S's return to grace since then, but this was the most important internal turning point.

The event not only shows the increasing importance of management development initiatives to the ability of any organization to carry through its strategy. It also shows how the nature of the function has changed. This event was not just about determining the new skills and knowledge managers at M&S would need, but how they would *feel* using them. It was as much about influencing behavior and attitude as laying down a process. And the event was not about imposing or gaining support for a pre-ordained change management program thought up by senior management – as had previously been the case at M&S – but inspiring and shaping managers' own ideas so they could be later endorsed by the Board.

What happened at M&S is also happening elsewhere. In 1996 the European Foundation for Management Development (efmd) in Brussels marked its anniversary by posing its members the question "What are we developing managers for?"

The efmd is a diverse organization with members that span political institutions, business schools and international corporations. By the mid-1990s, it had succeeded in recruiting not only senior HR managers and educationalists from the rich European Union states but also a wave of management development pioneers in Central and Eastern Europe, as the post-Communist world started to get to grips with Western styles of business.

Even given this, the feedback they received was extraordinarily eclectic. The list of capabilities and perspectives efmd members thought managers needed to acquire to do their jobs effectively would have taxed the most laterally minded MBA program designer.

There were plenty of references to the conventional management skills of the age: project management, team leadership, cross-functional collaboration. However, efmd members, representing 450 public and private sector organizations in 40 countries, also came up with a patchwork of other requirements that would not have featured on the hit list of a development program a decade before.

They spanned:

» the need to be *environmentally aware*: "Managers must develop their product design so that they can get an equally distributed production base around the world" (Italian environmental minister);
» the need to have *intuitive vision*: "I have to predict what is coming in an area I cannot see or understand" (Japanese chief executive of Minolta Europe);
» *lateral thinking*: "What we do at the General Electric corporate university at Crottonville is to offer new lenses to very bright competent people, whom we trust have a good understanding of what they need to know to be successful" (head of corporate leadership program, General Electric); and
» *metaphorical analogy*: "[MBAs at Harvard] create productive tensions by inviting people to challenge conventional views of any given subject by making the right contrasts and developing their own personal scenarios" (head of business school at Warsaw University).

The conclusion efmd reached is that in an age of rapid change and conflicting business philosophies, managers need to understand and champion *why* their organization exists as well as what needs to be done and the most efficient way of achieving it.

First, there is the increasing expectation that managers will be not just the servants of a pre-ordained business plan, but the *strategy* that lies behind it. This means working for the longer-term future of the business, not just today's targets and goals. It means commitment to the whole organization's success, not just to laid-down performance objectives. It means taking the initiative in identifying and exploiting new opportunities and, as the former chief executive of Minolta Europe put it at the efmd conference, handling the "unexpected and unthinkable."

Second, managers are increasingly being seen collectively as the key resource which influences the potential of the firm as a whole to respond to threats, exploit opportunities and change direction. In a recent interview for a British personnel journal, General Electric's pioneering former chief executive Jack Welch confirms this. "If your three or four top appointments at any level of the organization are good, you have won the game – if you bat 75%, you are doing a hell of a job."

This is confirmed by our own research for the UK management institute Roffey Park, which examines how groundbreaking business ideas are inspired, shaped and sustained (see Chapter 9). We found that line managers and supervisors are the key determiners of whether good ideas get taken up and developed. In many of the firms we surveyed, the challenge of innovation was seen to be by senior executives that not enough suggestions and insights on the ground are picked up and properly developed. It was not the lack of original thinking that was the problem. It was the fact that managers are not mandated to pick it up, recognize its value and champion its cause.

Managers do not therefore merely administer the organization they work for. They "engage" it, and what they engage is not just its resources but its collective soul. The challenge for management developers is that to enable them to fulfill this task, they have to develop new approaches and methods that will not only allow them to assess what they do as managers, but also how they think, feel and see their work – and, in turn, to help their subordinates undertake the same task.

Antonio Borges, dean of the European business school INSEAD between 1995 and 2001, comments:

"Many people recruit their managers in the hope they will become agents of change. This puts a lot of pressure on them and on us as management developers with regard to how we train and prepare them.

"This requires us, of course, to bring people to a level of knowledge and competence to physically run a work unit or organization. But there is also an increasing emphasis on personal and professional development that will help them to communicate, interact and motivate. These two objectives cannot be traded off against each other."

This ExpressExec guide will highlight how organizations, and the schools and consultants working with them, are meeting this challenge.

What is Management Development?

» The importance of context
» The importance of tailoring
» The importance of human interaction and its creative output

So how, like Marks & Spencer and General Electric, do you influence how managers think about their work? What they feel about it? The way they see it? How do you help them undertake that same task with their staff?

INSEAD's former dean Antonio Borges (see Chapter 1) defined the challenge in 1995:

"Managers are no longer people in control, but to a very large extent coaches. They do not focus so much on putting directly supervised systems into place, but on self-perpetuating processes. Above all they need to receive the signals that come from the market, from the competitors, and integrate them into a coherent approach that the company can use to make collective, intelligent decisions.

"This is very different from the management of 20 or 30 years ago. Yet we as management developers do not always take this new context into account in the type of programs that we offer. This requires our investing a great deal in understanding what is happening in the world of management; but in particular to translate this into the appropriate implications for our own programs and activities is an ambitious and difficult process."

Borges was addressing a largely commercial audience. The challenge for management developers in the public sector is even greater. This is because the relationship between government or state-run health and social services and the people they serve is infinitely more complex than that which exists between a company and its clients.

"I am not a mere customer of my government, thank you," says McGill University's Henry Mintzberg, author of the best selling *Rise and Fall of Strategic Planning*. "I expect something more than arm's length trading and something less than the encouragement to consume. I am a *citizen*, with rights that go beyond those of customers or even clients."

As a consequence, argues Mark Moore of Harvard's John F. Kennedy School of Government, public managers have to be even more opportunistic and adaptive than their private sector counterparts. "The thoughts, experience and imagination of public sector executives are a potentially valuable resource," he says. "If properly challenged, and effective management development is part of this process, they can be as valuable an engine to creating value in the public sector as they have been in the private."

Moore's point – that development is about challenging people, not indoctrinating them – helps to inform some basic principles about the purpose, design and execution of management training or education initiatives that, we argue, lie at the heart of successful HR practice in this field.

THE IMPORTANCE OF CONTEXT

It almost goes without saying that any learning, points of good practice, tools and techniques or expert knowledge that emerge from management development initiatives need to be transferable. However, the context in which managers from different organizations apply their skills is so diverse that this transferability needs to be explored thoroughly on the program, and even demonstrated in practice.

It is easy to see why this applies in the case of participants from different sectors. The argument presented by Professors Moore and Mintzberg about the public sector (see above) is a good case in point. Superficially, the skills needed by managers look the same. Moore's research into public sector management skills at the Kennedy School suggests that local government or health care managers are every bit as opportunistic, adaptive, self-sufficient and entrepreneurial as their private sector counterparts.

However, the context in which these skills are applied is so radically different as to make any direct lift of expertise or training from commercial courses at best unhelpful and at worst misleading. For example, the idea that government organizations are supposed to be responsive to *citizens* acting collectively through the machinery of democratic government is very different than the idea that government organizations are supposed to be responsible to individual *customers*.

If government organizations are supposed to be responsive to citizens acting collectively, then any local government officer cannot use his or her entrepreneurial skills to launch an initiative in the community using state funding – for example, an after-school program for latch-key children – until those citizens, acting collectively through their elected officials, signal that this service will not only benefit them as individual customers, but is also worthy of public support. He or she cannot act as a public manager until the public has said that the interests of the customer are *publicly* as well as *privately* valued.

A private manager, using commercially raised capital, would be under no such strictures in offering the same service. If something is valued by individuals to meet a local need, then the only consideration someone delivering that service needs to consider is whether he or she can offer it at a price that those individuals are prepared to pay at a margin that will provide a sustainable profit. No collective mandate is required or expected.

As Moore concludes:

"There has been an awful lot of loose talk about how the public sector can learn from the private in being 'responsive' and 'customer oriented.' But this fails to address what external demands government or health care managers should respond to and the techniques and transferable learning involved are only as valuable as the extent to which this different dynamic of accountability is factored into the learning."

Bending it like Beckham

But even commercial organizations have individual constraints and characteristics that have to be taken into account when using "off the shelf" techniques or approaches. As far back as 1989, a study by Dr Wendy Hirsh of the UK Institute for Employment Studies examined the basic vocabulary used by organizations to describe essential management skills. Not surprisingly, the most popular included communication, leadership, judgment, initiative, organizing and motivation.

However, when Hirsh explored what these words actually meant to managers, from one organization to the next, she found some startling contrasts. "Good decision making" meant "taking innovative decisions" in one company and "analyzing hard data and minimizing commercial risk" in another. "Managing risk" meant "being cautious about lending" in a high street bank and "taking calculated gambles and accepting the possibility of losses when there is a probability of significant gain" in an investment bank.

Exploring the real meaning of the organization's use of language is critical here. Professor Johan Roos of the International Institute for Management Development in Lausanne argues that companies are no more than "systems of language." The words used by senior managers to describe key management skills and, more importantly, the extent to which their interpretation of these phrases is shared by subordinates at each level of the organization, determine the dominant business culture.

The adaptability of this language to emerging events and circumstances also determines whether the organization will adapt well to change. Checking whether the underlying understanding of the skills and qualities used to define a management development assignment is shared by the participants and their own line managers is one of the key purposes of the organizational needs analysis that should ideally precede any design of delivery.

THE IMPORTANCE OF TAILORING

This does not mean that the only relevant approach to developing managers lies in in-company design or delivery, or that the only lessons worth disseminating come solely from the organization or its sector. Indeed, as we will discuss later on, it is of paramount importance that managers are exposed to new thinking and good practice from outside their immediate boundaries.

But it does mean that any generally applicable "intervention" on a management development initiative – whether it is a diagnostic model or tool, a teaching case or a presentation of a new business theory – needs to be framed in the context of the personal or organizational circumstances faced by the participants.

Suit you sir!

This is commonly achieved using a variety of methods, explored in more detail in Chapter 6, including:

» training needs analysis (TNA), both individual and collective;
» preparatory exercises that ensure participants begin the program with a compatible set of individual and collective objectives and with examples drawn from their own experiences;

» tailored exercises, scenarios, case examples, individual assignments and group work that takes the generic models, research, tools or theories and allows participants to explore how they apply at the very least in their own sector and preferably in their own organization;

» post-program literature, disseminated via a dedicated newsletter or intranet, which captures the output of these exercises or group work; and

» post-program reviews, either individual or collective, which assess how valuable the output of the program has proved.

THE IMPORTANCE OF HUMAN INTERACTION AND ITS CREATIVE OUTPUT

In 1997, the UK's Cranfield School of Management surveyed 1,200 of its alumni to find out what they found most valuable about taking part in the school's MBA and related postgraduate programs.

According to the report's author, Caroline Buller, they want to reproduce, in the executive courses they participate in, the same atmosphere of learning they experienced in MBA case or lecture discussions. They do not see these sessions as a one-way process but as a chance to test out their own ideas and theories with their peer group. Many feel that conventional executive education fails to capture this dynamic edge and is too focused on specialist interests. As Buller explains:

"What alumni are saying to us is this: 'Tell me something that I didn't know. Challenge me. Astonish me.' In the same way, if the session is led by a well-known professor, they do not want well-polished presentations based on his well-polished theories. They want him to explore dangerous territory and ideas on the cutting edge, where they can make their own contributions to emerging concepts and present while they emerge."

Our own experience is that this yearning for interactive creative energy is not confined to MBA alumni. Good initiatives work like ripples in a pond. You throw a stone into the water – a new theory, piece of research, tool or technique – and the learning is generated not by the stone itself but by the energy of the water responding to the impact.

Heart to heart

Exchanges between individuals attempting to answer the questions "Here is an interesting theory. What does it mean to me?" "What does it mean to you?" "What does it mean to the organization?" "How can we apply it?" places participants in the roles that our own research suggests lies at the heart of how ideas are created and developed.

The theory is merely the starting point or "spark." By acting out the roles of sponsor (champion of the idea), shaper (how does it apply here?) and sounding board (what constraints or considerations apply?), the participants – rather than the originator working on his or her own – take the theory and make it applicable to the organization. It is that output that often proves the most valuable collective and individual resource to the organization. Yet it is this output that often fails to be captured, as flipcharts, video snapshots and all the other by-products of a management course are literally or metaphorically placed on the back burner.

Share and share alike

In this sense, effective management development is not confined to inculcating new knowledge and expertise among participants but capturing their response. The comparison with MBA programs is again useful here. Prospective MBA graduates choose a program not just because of the faculty that will teach them but the students they will learn with. The response and reactions of a variety of practicing professionals whose perspective is shaped by different national upbringings, traditions and the experience of working in different industries is what gives a good MBA course its cutting edge.

Any management program is the same. The participants may not come from different countries or industries or even organizations – although in an increasingly global and networked business world this is increasingly the case, even in in-company programs. However, their responses to new theories and good practice will be shaped differently by other factors: their personal or professional education, their private interests, the work of their spouse, the unique culture of their work unit. Capturing that response and using it as a learning resource should be a primary role in any management developer's remit.

In da house?

This then raises the issue of who is placed to design and manage the process: the internal consultant who is closer to the organization's strategic needs or the external consultant or academic who has a better grasp of the material that will form the basis of the initiative.

There is probably no other branch of HR management that has been transformed so dramatically by the outsourcing revolution. No single model dominates. One polarity is where the internal HR practitioner, usually an expert in the field, conducts the organizational needs analysis, translates strategic or business needs into a program or course design, sources a mixture of internal line managers and external subject experts to work to this design under his or her direct supervision and subsequently undertakes the review or appraisal of what has been achieved.

This ideal has reached its most perfect ideal in the US-style corporate learning centers or "universities," pioneered by large North American corporations like Motorola and General Electric but now taken up by European companies including Banco Santander, Ahlstrom, Allianz-Versicherung and Cisco. We explore the role of these centers more fully in the next chapter.

At the other end of the spectrum is the smaller operation that contracts the whole process out to a consultancy or business school that has specialist client liaison and analysis expertise and the facilities needed to either host the initiative or coordinate it via a dedicated intranet. The HR manager in these circumstances acts as broker and procurer, reviewing and validating the design of the initiative but stepping back from direct delivery.

The majority of initiatives fall somewhere in between, depending on the expertise of the HR practitioner and the capabilities of the supplier. However, in all cases, the HR practitioner has to exercise significant consumer judgment in assessing and selecting the right suppliers and monitoring whether they are really adapting their resources to meet the brief or engaging in sleight of the hand, cosmetic tailoring of off-the-shelf materials or methods. The skills needed to undertake this are explored more fully in Chapter 6.

KEY LEARNING POINTS

» Effective management development is contextual. Skills and knowledge may be transferable but the way they need to be applied is not.

» Materials and design always need tailoring. This does not mean that managers should not be exposed to new ideas and methods. Far from it. But it does mean that their relevance and applicability to the individual's circumstances and the organization's goals need to be demonstrated.

» Human interaction is at the heart of any initiative. Good initiatives work like ripples in a pond. The energy is generated not by the stone you throw in but the way the water responds.

» Participants are the resource as well as the recipients. They learn from each other's responses and perspectives as much as from the original proposition. The outputs from their discussions, often wasted or ignored, are important sources of the new insights and firm-specific solutions.

» Externally sourced expertise needs to be matched by internal knowledge and insight. A good initiative often consists of a world-wise consultant briefed by a company-savvy HR practitioner.

Evolution of Management Development

» University management education: Liberal art or applied science?
» In-company training: Flying too high for comfort
» The world turned upside down: Management development in the 1990s
» The HR role: Filling a discerning trolley

The integrated model of management development described in the previous chapter is the product of a meeting of minds between experts in two related but mutually independent fields. The first is the field of management education, an activity principally undertaken by higher education institutes or management centers, targeted at individuals and providing transferable skills and knowledge that can be used across different organizations or sectors.

The second is the field of management training, an activity principally undertaken or supervised by internal HR practitioners and while targeted at individuals, providing firm-specific skills and knowledge that are intended to be used in the context of a specific firm or sector.

The bridge and recent synergy between these activities is not confined to management development. The new approach reflects similar changes in all fields of training and development and the impact of a number of forces during the past two decades, including the need for continuous professional education and lifelong learning, the growth in new learning technology and the requirement for individuals to be able to work across boundaries and cultures.

However, the roots and prejudices that influence the education and development of managers – and which are still very evident today – stretch back over a century and a half. As recently as 10 years ago, there was still no consensus about whether management education was an undergraduate or postgraduate university discipline, a branch of professional development or a form of on-the-job training. Since this still affects the methods and programs on offer to client organizations from a very wide range of suppliers, it is worth examining these origins in more detail.

UNIVERSITY MANAGEMENT EDUCATION: LIBERAL ART OR APPLIED SCIENCE?

Management education, like management itself, emerged from the technological revolution of the mid-nineteenth century. The expansion of the big utilities that transformed the Victorian era – railways, telegraph, cargo-based shipping, oil, electricity – changed business from the provenance of a small mercantile elite to a social engine of transformation employing millions. It created a new commercial structure, the limited liability company, to enable entrepreneurs to raise the capital they needed from large investors; and it created a new class of worker, the manager, to run the operation on a day-to-day basis while the owner focused exclusively on plans for expansion and the raising of new capital.

Nowhere did this transformation occur more quickly and more dramatically than in the United States between 1870 and 1930, as the nationally coordinated industrial forces unleashed by the Civil War boosted the science of mass manufacture and distribution.

"The business of America is business," said President Calvin Coolidge in 1925. The emergence of large corporations and trusts brought to an end the era of individual enterprise in the American economy. What Rockefeller's Standard Oil Company achieved in oil refining, Andrew Carnegie sought in steel and Pillsbury in flour milling.

Frederick Winslow Taylor, a Pittsburgh Quaker engineer, preached the gospel of "scientific management:" breaking complex skills down to their simplest components. The skilled worker who took 290 minutes to assemble a fly-wheel magneto at a Ford plant was replaced by an assembly line of men who took just 13 minutes for each item.

Yet the irony is that a new field that everybody at the time saw as a science wound up being taught at university as a liberal art – and it was this model of US management education that was exported to the rest of the non-Communist world.

Beware of Greeks bearing gifts

Academics had been giving thought to how to teach managers as early as the late 1860s. The former Confederate generalissimo Robert E. Lee, when appointed President of Washington College in 1867, argued that the traditional classical education provided by most higher education institutes was hopelessly inadequate to help them exploit its untapped potential.

Writing to a potential sponsor, he commented: "To you who are so conversant with the necessities of the country, and its vast undeveloped resources, the benefit of applying scientific knowledge and research to the management of agriculture, mining, architecture, construction, railroads, canals, bridges etc. will at once be apparent."

In 1880, after 15 years of sustained post-war growth, the first fully fledged department of management studies was established at the

University of Pennsylvania. The model established at the Wharton School, which was copied by its many successors, was however to study business almost wholly in abstract and from a largely clerical perspective. A conventional framework of undergraduate and postgraduate degrees was adopted, with postgraduates requiring no experience of management work and their work validated by a conventional thesis.

The curriculum of these new courses built on the original accounting and book keeping courses that came to be needed as the country lost its frontier image and began to industrialize. The Masters of Business Administration (MBA) program, which emerged at the turn of the century, was a two-year academic program and most students enrolled immediately after taking a first degree.

Ivory and ebony

This model was perfectly adequate during the heyday of Taylorism in the first half of the twentieth century. Every element of work was broken down to its simplest form and codified, workers were drilled according to the code, there was little need for leadership and still less for initiative. The model of management taught on MBA courses seemed vindicated by the Second World War when the assembly line methods pioneered by Henry Ford and Frederick Taylor gave the United States the industrial muscle she needed to out-manufacture Germany and Japan.

By the 1950s, however, both undergraduate and MBA programs were coming under attack from industry, both for an alleged lack of academic rigor and for providing little of relevance to current strategic business issues. Two reports on the state of American management education appeared in 1959. One was written by Robert A. Gordon and James E. Howell, both sponsored by the Ford Foundation, and the other by Frank C. Pierson, backed by the Carnegie Corporation. Both reports lambasted American graduate management education as little more than vocational colleges filled with second rate students taught by second rate professors who did not understand their fields, did little research and were out of touch with business.

The Carnegie and Ford reports landed like bombshells on the business schools sitting in the middle of university campuses and with pretensions to academic respectability. Their response was rapid.

Schools hardened their admissions standards and upgraded standards of teaching. They also established the now well-known American emphasis on academic research. As a result the classic US MBA program came into being – a first year of required "core" courses that provided a grounding in the basics of management and a second year of electives to allow specialization or deeper study.

It proved universally popular in North America and the US model has been exported all over the world. In 1958, at Fontainebleau in France, the European Institute of Business Administration (INSEAD) was set up, offering American style graduate programs. In the UK, following a report by Lord Franks in 1963, American style schools were set up, not in the hallowed halls of Oxford or Cambridge but in the altogether more matter-of-fact precincts of London and Manchester universities. In Asia, the Hong Kong University of Science and Technology was established in 1991 with faculty and financial help from the Andersen School at California's UCLA.

Yet for all this success, misgivings about the relevance of university business education to business needs have remained constant. Part of the problem lay in the reforms made in the wake of the Carnegie and Ford reports. The authors criticized business schools on two counts: they lacked academic rigor and they lacked business relevance. The measures taken by schools to respond to the first criticism, however, made it increasingly difficult for them to respond to the second.

The process became over-academic. Research was paramount. Chairs were granted, as in other university departments, on the basis of published contributions to refereed journals that became increasingly specialized, esoteric and cut off from business realities. This specialization also discouraged cross-functional collaboration at a time when, as a result of the total quality management revolution of the 1970s and 1980s, industry was breaking down functional boundaries and fostering teamwork. Sub-departments of the schools adopted feudal practices, ring fencing their own research and launching their own portfolio of specialist programs and courses, some of them linked to postgraduate qualifications, rather than contributing to the school's broader strategy for growth.

Schools would have been forced to reform their act far earlier had it not been for the explosion in demand for MBA graduates from the newly created management consultancies and investment houses, who cared little about what was taught on the curriculum and more about the recruitment caliber of student the schools were now attracting.

When a new wave of reforms occurred in the early 1990s it was because of a sudden dip in demand from the consultancies and finance houses, who now recruited three-quarters of all MBA graduates, and the thumbs down schools received when they tried to target industrial recruiters. To see why, we have to look at what was happening to internal management training over the same period.

IN-COMPANY TRAINING: FLYING TOO HIGH FOR COMFORT

Management training in the 1960s and 1970s was highly elitist. Only those deemed to be high flyer material were seriously invested in. The keys to these fast track strategies were:

» early selection, either through a graduate selection scheme linked to assessment centers and psychological testing; or through an internal scheme targeted at 25–30 year olds, using similar techniques;
» planned career progression, organized through a series of attractive projects and assignments, usually lasting about five years;
» planned succession planning, to ensure that promising high flyers appear regularly on the shortlist of upcoming senior posts; and
» placement of prestigious external management training courses at top business schools or, as an alternative, action learning programs – climbing mountains or fording rivers.

If the HR department's card-index system, planned promotion and luck worked in unison, then the lucky candidate would find himself (and in this era, it nearly always was a "him") within sight of senior management positions by his mid-thirties. At this stage, phase two of high flying took over and he was groomed for particular senior posts, usually by moving him between functions to broaden his business appreciation. If, at 35, the aspiring senior executive was stuck in a career blockage at the lower levels of management in a dead-end function (like personnel), he could safely assume that he was never a high flyer and that he must have done something wrong.

That Icarus feeling

The appeal of high flyer schemes was surprisingly deep seated. They helped the board alleviate their anxieties about the next generation of senior executives, by reassuring themselves that "something was being done." They profited from the career expectations of a new generation of baby-boomers leaving college. At a time when the structure of organizations was still vertical and silo-oriented, they held out the prospect that good people would not get "lost" and never reach the top. And they had a tremendous appeal to both personnel specialists and business school tutors, because they looked active and modern and provided lots of "fun" training activities with only small groups of bright participants.

Tom Glynn Jones, BP's manager of human resources in the late 1980s, explained the attraction in an interview conducted at the time for the British *Sunday Times*:

> "If, as in this country, you recruit your managers after their first degree and you want to get them to the top levels of management in time for them to be of any use, you have at most about 20 years. With the number of management levels they need to go through and the different range of experiences they will require, this is not a very long time."

BP's own scheme was state-of-the-art for the period. Managers were recruited to the scheme in their late twenties. "By this time they will have established their professional reputation in their chosen specialism and will already have a record of high performance," explained the then senior personnel officer in charge of the scheme, James Fischer. "Under the appraisal system operating throughout the company, it may be a year before the final decision is made in close consultation with the executive head of the candidate's group."

During managers' time on the program (5–10 years) their progress was overseen by a committee of 15 senior managers chaired by the head of one of BP's main operating companies. A sub-committee meeting twice a month worked with individual candidates and their managers to plot career moves and decide on appropriate training.

"We aim to provide them with a combination of depth and breadth," Fischer continued. "In addition to their existing professional base, we provide them with experience outside their own field, in another business or in a corporate activity. We also give them experience overseas, in a finance or planning role, and increasingly in information technology. Finally, they receive some formal business management training, usually in a prestigious management school."

On completion of the program, candidates transferred to a senior executive preparation course supervised by a committee chaired by the corporation's deputy chairman. This program was undertaken by all BP's executives from divisional manager upwards.

At the time, this fast track strategy provided BP with more than half of its senior executives and a similar proportion of boardroom directors. Tom Glynn Jones saw it as one of the chief contributors to the quality of BP's management.

THE WORLD TURNED UPSIDE DOWN: MANAGEMENT DEVELOPMENT IN THE 1990S

By the end of the 1980s, however, most of the economic conditions on which high flying schemes thrived had been transformed. Steady growth, the ability to offer a job for life and relatively unchanging markets had all disappeared. In the process, some of the basic assumptions of conventional fast track development – that management potential can be spotted early on, that the definition of this potential will still be relevant in 20 years' time when young managers reach the top, that career moves can be planned and achieved well in advance and that effective leadership from the top is all that is needed to keep an organization competitive – were seriously under question.

In addition, longer term forces were at work. Regardless of fluctuations in the growth rate of individual countries, the following global factors were to turn upside down the conventions of post-Second World War management development.

Clone for clone's sake

The mechanisms for spotting executive talent are often self-fulfilling. Selected early on, the candidate and everyone else think he is wonderful.

A homogenous senior management team results. As established company after established company went to the wall or plunged from grace in the early 1990s because senior managers failed to spot decisive shifts in the market, the consequences became apparent. Diversity rather than homogeneity became the essential asset for survival and the need to maintain a pool of talent varied in both size and nature the best means to achieve it.

In addition, responsiveness to change requires a different philosophy of leadership. At a lecture in 1990, Harvard's John Kotter commented: "Major change always demands more leadership. Consider a simple military analogy. A peacetime army can usually survive with good administration up and down the hierarchy, A wartime army, however, needs competent leadership at all levels. No one has figured out how to manage people into battle; they must be *led*."

I'm leader, what now?

The leader for different and devolved leadership was accentuated by the total quality revolution. Specialist managers were now responsible not only for developments in their own area of operations, but also for linking their functions to other parts of the business. To achieve their objectives they now had to be team players, able to lead and coach their subordinates using a complex array of interpersonal skills and to cooperate with their colleagues in other business units using negotiation and persuasion.

The ability to lead complex multidisciplinary projects – one seen solely as a prerequisite in construction, oil exploration and civil engineering – was now seen as an essential skill for all managers. A new vocabulary of management roles accompanied the cutting of business layers by half or even two-thirds: networking, gatekeeping, pulsetaking, stakeholder management, sponsoring and resource gathering.

Physician, heal thyself?

The need for continuous development was not only devolving downwards. It was traveling into the boardroom. Pioneers of better corporate governance like Bob Garratt and Manfred Ket de Vries (see Chapter 8) argued that specialists appointed as directors would fail to rise above the daily round of operations to see the changes taking place in their industries and sectors, unless some formal intervention was made by an HR or academic expert.

"Directors are rarely given any induction into their new role or inclusion into their work teams," warned Garratt in 1988. "No time or money is usually made available for them to develop themselves into their direction giving role, so that after a six- to nine-month struggle, feeling very uncomfortable in the process, they do what any person would do and return to their previous position of specialist comfort. As a consequence, there is not enough time or diversity of thinking going into the direction-giving policies and strategies of the organization."

At the same time, corporate governance has moved from being a subject that most front line managers think more boring than watching paint dry to a major boardroom concern. Institutional investors, who by the late 1980s owned three-quarters of the equitable stock of publicly owned companies worldwide, shifted from expressing their concern about how firms were managed by dumping their stock (Doing the Wall Street Walk) to actively intervening in shaping how the board is run.

Whether the roles of chairman and chief executive are split, how non-executive directors are selected and inducted, how audit and recruitment sub-committees are supervised and monitored and how boardroom pay is determined have all featured on their hit list. Whether the institutions making the running are state-run pension boards (as in the United States) or private insurance firms (as in the UK), their change stance on corporate governance concerns has opened up a whole new industry in boardroom development.

The Venus de Milo factor

All people have careers that reach certain levels by certain ages. In conventional management career structures, the ages of 30–35 are particularly important. This leads to a high incidence of stress in young managers. It is also the reason why successful high flyers are so often men.

The glass ceiling rule of thumb – that women will not reach senior management unless they choose between career and family – sparked a revolution in new work patterns. But it quickly became evident that offering job sharing, home working and career breaks would benefit aspiring women part-timers little unless they had access to the same development opportunities as their full-time counterparts.

As Val Hammond, chief executive of the UK's Roffey Park Institute, commented in the early 1990s:

> "In terms of formal training, it is at this stage [middle management] that women's participation falls away and this may be linked to the fact that this is the level at which women tend to plateau.
>
> "They may be 'parked' here for some years, usually more than men, and they may leave. This may be to join another firm, to start their own business, for family reasons, or to study for further qualifications. This stage seems to carry with it an element of self-fulfilling prophecy in that if women do not receive clear signals from the company about their career potential, then they are acting perfectly rationally in deciding to leave even though this may then confirm the company's fear that they were a poor risk."

Touch me, feel me ...

The constraints surrounding management training, which until recently had to be delivered on-site and face to face, have been practically eliminated by the almost universal take-up of e-mail, intranet and Internet working.

The first breakthrough in distance learning occurred as early as the 1970s when a combination of television, video and audio tape technology made it possible for self-paced and home-based learning to extend well beyond the sterile correspondence courses that up until then had occupied a rather seedy, second place in the options open to mature students.

However, this intermediate process did not allow for group work and team synergy which, as we have already seen, became a priority for managers in an era of delayering and devolution. Providers of distance learning, like the UK's Open University and Henley Management College, linked distance learning modules with summer or project-based courses that brought participants together to conduct face to face the interactive element of management training that fostered interpersonal and planning skills.

The Internet revolution, accompanied by new breakthroughs in brainstorming and discussional database software, has made it possible for the first time for sophisticated team exercises to be carried out by participants around the world. There is some evidence to suggest that work carried out this way can be even more productive, in terms of ideas and insights, than training carried out face to face.

Nonetheless, the technology is way in advance of people's ability to assimilate it. A considerable debate has opened up in the first decade of the twenty-first century over the extent to which advanced management development initiatives can be conducted and delivered over the Net; and where and in what circumstances face to face sessions are still integral to the tacit learning that is so important to organizational learning or networking. This debate is covered in more depth in the next chapter.

You are how you manage

Perhaps the most important precursor to the management development agenda we enjoy today is the breakthrough in strategic thinking brought about by the organizational competence and learning movement.

The first concepts of change management, promulgated by academics like Harvard's John Kotter and London Business School's Charles Handy in the early 1980s, centered on the entrepreneurial leader's capacity to motivate or remotivate the organization through an original vision and a clear strategy to achieve it. Drawing on the example set by a new breed of younger iconoclastic owner managers like The Body Shop's Anita Roddick, Virgin's Richard Branson and "raspberry rebel" ice cream makers Ben and Jerry, this launched a new wave of interest in individual leadership programs and initiatives.

However, in the early 1990s, independent thinkers like Gary Hamel, Richard Pascale and Meredith Belbin started to stress the importance of "organizational competence." The essence of their strategy is that, at a time when loyalty, retention and motivation are at a premium, an organization's ability to tap the collective knowledge and skills of its workers provides it with its key competitive edge.

For the first time, the idea that an organization's ability to survive and thrive is dependent largely on the vision and creativity of the senior management team has been challenged. The cognitive and technical potential lies in the workforce. The role of the senior manager is to find, foster, develop and sustain it.

This turns on its head the traditional premise of high flying management development. In an age when jobs for life and life-long loyalty in business have gone for good, elitist management development strategies are short-sighted not only because they place the organization's future in a small group of individuals whose very premium will result in their swift departure; but because investing a limited development budget in this group of princelings is nearly always at the expense of a wider underdeveloped management workforce.

As Roffey Park's Wendy Hirsh comments:

> "For every Icarus that is turned on by a high-flyer scheme, there are 10 other managers (or potential managers) who are not. Telling a small part of the workforce it has talent appears very like telling the rest that they lack it. Even if the scheme is supposed to be confidential, employees are not blind."

A buyer's market

By the late 1980s, it was becoming clear that the model of management education implemented in the wake of the US Carnegie and Ford reports was too rigid and elevated to meet the evolving needs of employers. Individual academic departments, covering functional specialisms like marketing, finance and operations, operated in silos. There was little or no incentive for ambitious academic experts to collaborate or experiment as the criteria for promotion depended on specialist rather than generalist knowledge. In addition, the schools' most prestigious output, MBAs, were being recruited in large numbers of consultancies and investment houses who were more interested in their analytical and intellectual abilities than what they were taught on the program.

It is no coincidence that when the necessary curriculum reforms came, in the early 1990s, it was at a time when the demand for MBAs from consultancies and finance houses took a temporary but dramatic dip and schools were caught with their pants down. In a short but intense period of debate and experimentation, between about 1989 and 1994, a completely new management development industry was born.

The first benefit was new-look MBA programs. Traditional programs, led by Wharton, UCLA and London, were revamped with greater emphasis being placed on cross-functional tasks like managing quality, globalization and project management. In Europe, schools like INSEAD and IMD fine-tuned existing one-year programs that made it easier for older managers to take time off for postgraduate study in mid-career. In the UK, in tandem with a disastrous attempt by the Management Charter Initiative to lever management education into a framework of professional qualifications – a square peg in a round hole if ever there was one – a select group of institutions pioneered consortium and in-company programs that linked academic assignments with key projects at work.

More importantly, a genuine consumer marketplace was created in which a diverse range of university business schools, independent management centers and specialist consultancies competed to meet very specific niches of demand. Teamworking, project management, leadership (at all levels), innovation management, boardroom education, family business development, benchmarking, organizational learning projects and internal venturing are some of the many services on offer – requiring HR practitioners to develop and apply strict criteria assessment procedures which are explored in greater depth in Chapter 6.

This market is now well developed, but there are still rigidities that require very careful management by internal HR practitioners to overcome. The first is the ability of suppliers to tailor materials, research and techniques to the needs of particular clients. In the United States, the failure by university schools to meet the specific needs of their clients led to large corporations like Motorola, Dupont and General Electric to set up their own corporate learning centers – a move now taken up elsewhere in the world by counterparts like Toyota, NatWest, Unipart, Ericsson, Cap Gemini and Heineken. Smaller clients who lack the resources or expertise to follow this route can nonetheless develop a series of measures to take the expertise of the external market and "frame" it in the context of their managers' work. This is also explored in greater depth in Chapter 6.

Linked to this is the failure of business schools and consultancies to develop new approaches for specific industries or sectors. Laura

Tyson, current dean of the London Business School and former dean of the Hass School at Berkeley, CA, recently commented that the inability of business schools to develop appropriate management models and development strategies for public services like health or transport was because the expertise and research needed was simply not available.

Modern business schools, although they often form part of a university campus, are strictly commercial animals. Their ability to originate research that will inform and resource new programs and initiatives is almost dependent on private funding and the availability of academics who perceive that there is sufficient consultancy work in the slipstream to justify the upfront investment of time needed to conduct the research.

Thus it is no coincidence that the European schools that have developed research and consultancy services aimed at family businesses, like Switzerland's IMD and Spain's IESE – come from a part of the continent where family-owned or -run businesses are substantial corporations with the right internal expertise to foster long term research – rather than in the UK, where family businesses are generally small start-ups with poorly developed HR functions and little time or money to spend on anything but the most basic skills training.

Similarly, London Business School's efforts to develop a management model appropriate for professional partnerships was hampered by a lack of internal HR expertise and sponsorship – only law firms responding with the necessary money to fund comprehensive research.

THE HR ROLE: FILLING A DISCERNING TROLLEY

The role of the HR practitioner is therefore one of enlightened consumer. Expertise in all areas of technique and approach is not required. But an accurate feel for the real (rather than the perceived) needs of the organization is, as well as the ability to assess whether the services on offer can be adapted to meet the need.

Buy one, get one free

The differences between the services offered by a university school, an independent management center or a specialist consultant are subtle, but crucial. The trade-off between original expert knowledge or technique and the ability to analyze and adapt this expertise to the specific needs of the client may mean that an HR practitioner adopt a limited role in one initiative and a greatly expanded one in another.

Steven Kerr, Vice President of Corporate Leadership Development at General Electric in 1996, put it this way:

"Medical science has been around far longer than management science. Yet when you go to a doctor because you have symptoms, no competent doctor would say 'I don't need to examine you, take these pills. They are great.' It's the same with management science. When a consultant knocks on your door and says 'I don't know you, but I know I can help you,' slam that door as fast as you can. Whatever the technique or method, it cannot be so strong and so powerful that it connects to everybody's needs without some co-production or adaption."

In the next few chapters, we will examine the issues you will face and the good practice you will need to develop to make the balance (see Table 3.1).

Table 3.1 Timeline: The evolution of management development theory and practice.

Timescale	Prevalent theory or practice	Key thinkers
Late nineteenth century	*Management as a university discipline*: The emergence of large-scale utilities manufacturing leads to the emergence of a new profession	Frederick Wharton, founder of the Wharton School of Management at the University of Pennsylvania
Early twentieth century	*Management as a science*: The breakdown of work into tasks, and tasks into separate movements, in order to foster maximum efficiency	F.W. Taylor, Frank and Lillian Gilbreth

Table 3.1   (*continued*)

Post-war period	*Management as an elite cadre*: Hierarchy leads to "fast track" development schemes designed to spot and develop young talent early enough to leapfrog them through the career ladder	Wendy Hirsh, Lynda Gratton, Val Hammond, Rosabeth Moss Kanter
Late twentieth century	*Management as a Masters qualification*: Reforms prompted by the Ford and Carnegie foundations leads to a golden age of postgraduate business programs designed to turn specialists into generalists; an over-emphasis on academic standards and research, however, leads to a new breed of programs in the 1980s and 1990s sponsored, designed or delivered by corporations	
Early twenty-first century	*Management as a generator of learning and innovation*: A bottom-up dynamic shapes how people see, feel and think about their work as well as what they do; development becomes a collective process, generating new insights and firm-specific techniques as well as a common vision of the future	Peter Senge, Chris Argyris, John Burgoyne, Gary Hamel, Peter Honey

KEY LEARNING POINTS

» Management education, like management itself, emerged in the late nineteenth century as trading companies financed and run by owner managers gave way to publicly owned corporations run by professional intermediaries. Many of its key concepts still lie firmly rooted and shaped by the needs of limited liability companies whose most important stakeholders are investors rather than customers, employees or users.

» Given this, the most important work undertaken by both HR practitioners and business school academics in recent years has been to adapt management theories and the good practices that underpin them to the needs of other organizations – SMEs, non-profit making bodies and government agencies among others.

» It has never been uniformly agreed whether management is a profession, a science, a function or a liberal art. The formal preparation managers receive varies according to which view the provider or sponsor subscribes to. The view sponsored by the Carnegie/Ford corporations in the 1950s that regardless of its nature, it should be taught as a university discipline, has irrevocably shaped its delivery ever since.

» Until the last two decades, internal management development focused on getting a small number of individuals in the early part of their working lives up a long and tortuous career ladder. More recently, thanks to new concepts and competition in learning, it has focused more on using programs and initiatives as a focus for collectively achieved consensus and original thought across the whole organization.

» The delivery of management has been significantly outsourced over the same period. A new marketplace has emerged made up of providers with contrasting capabilities, including university business schools, independent management centers and specialist consultancies of all sizes. HR practitioners need to acquire expert and regularly updated consumer knowledge to buy in the right support.

The E-Dimension

» Fumbling at arm's length
» It's the blend that counts
» Fronting up
» Stewed or brewed
» To boldly go . . .

No debate in HR management is hotter than that of e-learning. At its heart is a very simple question. How many of the basic functions of learning – intellectual understanding of a concept or technique, ability to relate and apply it to your own work, ability to apply it in teams or projects – require the tacit interaction of face to face contact with a tutor and/or fellow participants; and how many can be conducted at a distance?

In turn, this centers around two factors that also determine the debate on any aspect of e-commerce: the technology available and the capacity of individuals to assimilate it. The two are almost never in tandem with each other. Professor Gareth Morgan of Toronto's Schulich School argues that truly personal and collaborative learning at a distance is now possible with "third generation" e-mail technology (see Table 4.1) but not achievable in reality either because organizations lack the necessary software; or, more importantly, because management systems are still predicated solely on delivering the learning capabilities of first or second generation technology.

When looking at how you can upgrade HR approaches to truly interactive learning, it is also worth bearing in mind that there is very little similarity from one person to the next in what influences individuals' capacity to assimilate technology. Age can be a factor, but it is not the be all and end all. The type of work you are engaged in, whether you use the technology at home, whether you have children that do, whether your psychological capacity to cope with change is well-developed or poor, are all determinants (see Table 4.1).

So are the signals and feedback you receive from managers and colleagues at work. This was the overwhelming conclusion of a study recently carried by Fiona Lee, an assistant professor of psychology at the University of Michigan who, with two colleagues from Harvard Business Review, looked at how hidden assumptions undermined a new technological initiative at a Midwestern healthcare organization.

The organization had recently introduced a Website that would provide medical staff and administrators with a single access point for retrieving the most up-to-date clinical information. Because there was no formal training course for the system, employees had to experiment with it to gain proficiency.

Table 4.1 Three generations of e-learning technology and their impact. Source: Professor Gareth Morgan, York University (Toronto, 2001).

First generation	Instructor driven, and simply understood as e-training: traditional courses and text put online and typically organized in a linear fashion
Second generation	Learner driven, self-organizing and evolving, and capable of being accessed at any point for "just in time" learning and "as needed" basis; simply understood as e-learning, but using today's limited range of Internet media and so delivering a narrow range of sensory stimulation and interactive capabilities
Third generation	Learner driven, built on "second generation" broadband platform with advanced interactive technology using a full range of media giving a richly interactive experience, with text, voice, pictures, movement delivered across the Net – requiring more advanced software and bandwidth than most have today
The e-impact	*2001's corporate reality*
» Cost reduction	» Being achieved frequently
» Improved accessibility	» As above
» Increased quality	» Not there yet, in many cases
» Personal, collaborative	» Just beginning
» Learning at a distance	

In a survey of 688 staff – covering five teaching hospitals, 30 health-care centers and 120 outpatient clinics – Lee and her colleagues assessed how each person was using the technology and how this use was influenced by the management culture in their work. She found that individuals were more willing to experiment with the new system – trying out different software applications and testing new system features – when their managers did two things: stated explicitly that making mistakes would be okay, and refrained from punishing employees over errors.

Managers who gave mixed signals, such as verbally encouraging experimentation while keeping in place a reward system that punished failure, created mistrust and confusion. The effects of inconsistent messages was particularly strong among junior staff. Medical students, for example, assumed that failed experiments would harm their careers because of the need to demonstrate their competence in front of their peers in order to win advancement. By contrast, Lee found employees who were "allowed the room to fail" ended up being the most proficient and satisfied with the new technology – and the quickest to integrate it into their everyday work.

FUMBLING AT ARM'S LENGTH

The relationship between learning and technology is therefore very complex and highly individual. This conclusion had already been driven home by the lessons learned by tutors and trainers during the revolution wrought by the precursor to e-learning, the distance learning initiatives that arose out of advances in video and audio tape technology during the 1970s.

Distance learning packages – a combination of interactive text illustrated by cases presented on video or audio tapes – theoretically provided a substitute for face to face lectures and case presentations in a classroom setting.

They failed to yield the breakthrough expected because the schools and HR practitioners who designed and wrote the material ignored the fact that a new medium requires a new language; and that, as Chris Argyris stresses in his theories on double loop learning, basic concepts acquired through private study need to be reinforced by interaction and feedback from tutors and fellow-students.

"Many universities and colleges in the 1970s and 1980s produced materials of such unspeakable tedium and poor quality that they proved to be a disincentive to learning," says Aldwyn Cooper, an early pioneer of distance learning for both the UK's Open University and Henley Management College. "It is a fallacy to believe that experts in a subject are necessarily capable of communicating their skills and knowledge to others. The fundamental lesson we learned from the early experiments in distance learning is that most lecturers in education, where research is prized above practical achievement, are incompetent communicators and that their material, however valuable and original, needs translation if it is to be understood in a medium outside the classroom."

Cooper argued that the failure to build distance learning into a broader framework of tuition stems from the fact that schools unaccustomed to new technology saw it as a superannuated version of correspondence courses – and resourced it accordingly.

"Schools that saw this kind of open learning as a cheap alternative to classroom teaching failed to grasp the potential of the technique," he says. "Even the best-designed and written materials will fail if the learner is not motivated to learn by continuous reinforcement and feedback. Too often, trainers on distance learning programs were those who had failed at other tasks rather than the school's best faculty who still looked down on these initiatives as second class."

IT'S THE BLEND THAT COUNTS

The lessons from these early mistakes were still being assimilated when the Internet burst into the office in the early 1990s. The availability of a new generation of intranet and discussional database software opened up new possibilities for distance learning. The potential for interactive discussion and feedback between the individual and the tutor and, equally important, between the individual and other participants on the program, seemed to provide the essential foundation for double loop learning that had been so conspicuously absent in the early initiatives.

However the capacity of people to establish the kind of trusting working partnerships that arise from close physical proximity was still in its infancy. As we have already seen from the research carried out by Michigan's Fiona Lee, the "comfort factor" of people engaged in intense and often intimate exchanges over the Net is neither consistent nor easily influenced.

The constraints had already been vividly illustrated in the field of marketing and service provision. In their 1994 book *Blown to Bits: How the New Economics of Information Transforms Strategy*, authors Philip Evans and Thomas Wurster emphasize that there is a play-off in meeting customers' expectations between "access:" the ease with which they can access service in any location at any time;

and "richness:" the quality of the relationship that is established with the customer once contact is made.

In a lecture about the new economy made at London Business School in 2001 Eric Salama, group strategy director of the marketing services group WPP, used the analogy to describe changes in the financial services industry. Customers who would have insisted on conducting market research or simple transactions face to face 10 years before are now quite happy to do so over the Net. However, in any transaction involving deeper trust, direct eye-balling is still essential.

"If I am a well-heeled professional with a stock portfolio that requires careful managing, and trust in the individual is a key factor in my choice of firm, it is a different matter entirely," Salama argues. "I will want to get a feel for the managers' know-how and integrity and this, at least for the moment, requires regular face to face contact. This is because my assessment is as likely to be influenced by the tacit signals I receive through his body language and eye contact as what he says or offers."

In the same way, most of the computer-driven distance learning programs in the early 1990s started from the firm stance that the new possibilities for virtual assignments conducted by groups of participants in different locations could only be effectively realized if individuals on the program had been first bonded together in face to face sessions.

A good example was the international in-company MBA program run by Henley Management College for Standard Chartered Bank (also explored in Chapter 5). In the first intake, in 1991, 18 managers from 12 countries took part, ranging from the chief financial officer in Tokyo and the senior strategic officer in Hong Kong to branch managers in Sidcup, UK, and Kuala Lumpur, Malaysia.

Participants were provided with a laptop computer to help them communicate with each other, their tutors and in-company trainers through Henley's global conferencing system. All academic materials, background reading, individual assignments and group tasks undertaken by a series of study groups, to which all participants were assigned, were conducted using this medium.

"The holy grail for us was to bring about an imaginative interaction between participants which leads to effective problem solving, decision making and the development of new ideas," says Dominic Swords, the designer of the program. "New technologies such as groupware, discussion databases and the Internet increase the sense of intimacy between ourselves and the participants. They have replaced more bureaucratic forms of communication which have made it hard to maintain the sharing process when participants are dispersed in different parts of the world."

Critical to the design, however, were residential seminars that brought the group together once a year in Hong Kong, Kuala Lumpur and the UK. Each study group also met at least once a quarter. Dominic Swords stresses that the degree of intimacy participants sustained over the Internet was possible only because of the ties that were made during the residential courses:

"We use these courses to undertake teambuilding and cross-cultural work, including outdoor training. The lesson we are learning again and again is that sophisticated learning over the Web can only be fostered through a face to face encounter."

FRONTING UP

That was 10 years ago. But this is rapidly shifting field. As WPP's Eric Salama comments, both customers' and employees' perceptions of what constitutes "richness," and whether this requires human or online contact to inspire or sustain it, is changing all the time.

"We anticipate that in a few years time it may be possible to provide a high level of richness, in terms of trusting business relationships, using technological means. For example we have a stake in a company that is developing sophisticated voice-over and video-over technology that will enable me to conduct visually satisfying conversations with, say, my asset manager or legal advisor.

"It still may be important for me to meet the individual at least to establish his or her credentials, but after that the technology will serve; and, hey, in an age when people get married over the Net without having even met each other, the initial meeting may prove less important over time. The key for any business is assessing consistently the expectation customers and employees have in terms of richness and how it is delivered and whether these expectations are ahead or behind the company's technology and what it can offer."

STEWED OR BREWED

So, in what is now termed "blended learning" – a combination of Internet-based and face to face training – how is the blend likely to change in terms of the key functions of management program design and delivery?

Assimilation and familiarity with basic management concepts

The longest established of all functions capable of being delivered at a distance – arguably dating as far back as the old correspondence course techniques. Considerably refined by better interactive writing and design by pioneers of 1980-style distance learning, the possibilities have reached a new peak with advanced internally commissioned intranet design.

The UK's arts and niche entertainment channel Channel 4, for example, uses sophisticated e-learning software to induct its new professional staff. Channel 4 is unique in the UK in being the only public sector organization that has to generate its own income and also unusual in that it does not produce any films or programs itself.

The role of the managers who commission the programs from independent production companies is therefore of critical importance. This not only covers interpreting the corporation's broadcasting strategy and policy but determining fees and intellectual property rights as well as checking that the contracts meet the legal requirements of current government legislation.

This summary of the corporation's functions provides the focus for a new interactive intranet site launched in 1999, designed to familiarize new staff to the commissioning department who may not have experienced anything like this before. Sheila Robertson, then head of the channel's organizational development team, brought in e-learning software consultancy IQdos to design the training modules.

On its recommendation she commissioned KMA Interactive Media to set up the intranet.

Robertson told KMA she wanted a product that would "turn heads" in terms of improving skills and communication. This, it responded, would necessitate a wide ranging hardware upgrade, so the channel started installing new systems. A new post was created in the organizational development so that one person could dedicate all their time to e-learning and the intranet.

The result has not only catapulted the HR department from the fringes of the organization to the center, but also broken new ground in creating self-paced intranet exercises that are fun as well as informative. Most popular of all has been a snakes and ladders game dreamt up by the business affairs department as a way of helping new recruits in the commissioning department to understand what it does.

A typical question in the game is:

> You are commissioning editor for Channel 4 television. A product company asks you whether it can set up a Website to accompany the program you are buying from it. Do you: (a) say that it's fine; (b) pass the query on to your business executive; or (c) e-mail Channel 4's interactive department, saying that the production company has the online rights for the series?
>
> Move forward three paces if you chose (b). Move back two paces if you didn't.

Jenny Tucker, assistant business affairs executive, was the contact point between the department and IQdos. The exercise is not, she argues, merely a cosmetic ice-breaker. The process of negotiating intellectual property rights is becoming more complicated and mistakes in the commissioning process can mean that the corporation loses the rights to the programs it wants to make.

Individual assignments and private research

This aspect of distance learning was very one-dimensional under the old correspondence course methods but achieved new interactive capabilities when mixed media open learning pioneers like the Open University and Henley Management College came onto the scene.

Private research was even more problematic. Even when interactive learning had been enhanced by video and audio tape cases and multi-choice self-paced exercises, distance learning as recently as the mid-1990s was still heavily dependent on individual students having access to a local business library or dedicated learning center. In Hong Kong during this period, for example, a survey by the British Council found that less than half of the students on distance learning programs had access to a suitable library, seriously undercutting the number who completed their studies.

Internet and intranet technology changed all this. Henley was quick to incorporate electronic access to a comprehensive database into all its executive and postgraduate distance learning programs. "All the reading material is now on CD-ROM," says Ian Turner, director of the MBA program. "Teaching, projects and learning assignments are prepared by faculty and delivered and assessed online. And there is online access to the library and databases."

Nor is this service confined to individual business school students. Both the Swiss school IMD and Britain's Cranfield School of Management are developing their own electronic learning "portals," through which managers working for their corporate clients can access their resources and expertise. At a recent conference on lifelong learning, Xavier Gilbert, a business strategy professor at IMD, said the school envisaged itself as a continuing source of knowledge for members of its corporate network and was setting up a variety of channels to make this happen.

Group assignments and brainstorming

The jury is still out on whether creative group interaction is achievable online. A rearguard of academic experts argue that the tacit language brought about by face to face contact is still essential as a first-base foundation, but there is a growing body of evidence to suggest that this is no longer the case.

Recent tests of new software designed to support electronic brainstorming by researchers at the Massachusetts Institute of Technology, involving 800 participants, found that electronic brainstorming sessions were more productive than sessions using traditional face to face methods. These productivity gains increased with the size of the group taking part. The more formal mechanisms imposed by brainstorming software ensure that less assertive members of the team are not crowded out or inhibited by participants with more forceful personalities.

Similarly, early experiments with videoconferencing technology by the branded food and drinks company Grand Metropolitan (now merged with Guinness in the Diageo corporation) found that global task forces set up to examine how GrandMet could better expand its presence in emerging markets were as productive at a distance as they would have been in the room.

"There was a slight loss of interaction. You do not feel like you are touching or feeling the person on the screen," says the director of management development who facilitated the meetings. "But because the meeting is more structured, it gives everyone a fair chance to have their say. No one dominates. You respect someone, you listen to them, you process what they say and you respond. You are better able to agree to an agenda and stick to it."

Inspirational teaching

The consensus is that this is the one area of training and development most resistant to online delivery. This is not to say that technology has no place in the classroom or training center. As the dean of New York's Stern Business School, George Daley, comments:

"Teachers are able to use more imaginative and sophisticated graphics. Students are able to use laptop computers linked directly to lecture desks and are able to conduct sophisticated exercises using spreadsheets. Management case-studies are conducted directly on computer and outside the classroom all students are connected using the World Wide Web."

However, the task of winning hearts and minds is still seen as a job for the inspirational teacher with students sitting at his or her feet. As Michael Earl, professor of informational technology at London Business School, puts it: "Technology can substitute the dissemination of expert knowledge, but it cannot reproduce the evangelical process of a creative individual who paints a picture of a promised land and charts a road that helps managers reach it."

Even the godfather of microchip technology, Intel's former president Andy Grove, concurs. Asked at London Business School, while giving a lecture, whether he would ultimately be replaced by a computer in his part-time role as a visiting lecturer at Stanford University, Grove surprised everyone. He argued that teaching was one of the few areas of professional activity where the current degree of human interchange was beyond technology's reach. "Teaching requires a level of mutual trust and empathy that is timeless," he said. "In this, it is second only to making love."

"Of course, at the start of the last century, they made the same pessimistic forecasts about conversations over the telephone," says WPP's Eric Salama (see above). "Telephone technology had to get to the stage where you could make direct calls yourself on the spur of the moment, and people had to get used to the fact that you could talk to a disembodied voice, but it happened. At the moment, videoconferencing technology is in its infancy and you cannot really look someone in the eye. But the upcoming systems are removing the inconsistency and there is no telling what people will feel is perfectly natural in another 20–30 years' time."

TO BOLDLY GO ...

Salama has the final word. This is a rapidly changing field and the pace – and therefore what is "technically" possible – is getting faster all the time. The initiative of which this book is part is a good example. When Oxford-based publisher Capstone decided to launch an electronic database of basic management concepts that companies or individuals could subscribe to, ExpressExec, the directors envisaged that most of the good practice would stem from research by external experts.

On launching, however, it very quickly became clear that an unexpected by-product of the Website – its ability to be customized and integrated into existing company intranet systems – was that it could be used to tap and record the wealth of tacit knowledge and good practice that lay hidden among the flipcharts, notes and braincells of a client's own workers.

"We were able to use the software to identify and record who the internal experts were in any given field – building brand equity, operations and technology, managing public affairs etc. – and enable them to field questions from anyone in the organization as well as the external experts we commissioned to develop the original materials," says Edward Lound, Capstone's e-development manager. "The questions and answers from these exchanges could then be re-worked into concepts and solutions that are unique to the company. These often matched, in quantity and quality, those provided from outside the company."

Watch this space.

CASE STUDY: NEWS INTERNATIONAL

Chris Dennis, co-designer of a "blended" learning initiative at News International, publisher of leading UK newspapers like *The Times*, *The Sunday Times* and the *Sun*, argues that its beauty is that it allows people a choice of how to learn and the freedom to pick the one that suits them best.

In the spring of 2000, News International was looking to update and revitalize its in-company certificate in management, aimed at junior and middle managers. For a number of years, the program had followed the traditional "workshop-workbook" format but, with attendance falling, the content and design needed a significant overhaul.

The company turned to an external consultancy, Worldwide Learning, to re-design the program and inject some new ideas. The design team made two fundamental changes. First, they broke down the existing program into its constituent parts, testing them with a cross-section of training professionals from within the business. Then, having identified the most appropriate delivery mechanism for each part, the team revised the underlying teaching theory to give learners much more responsibility for their own learning.

The revamped News International program comprises 12 modules, each covering a core element of management, from building and leading teams to financial management. The number of workshops has been reduced from 36 half days to 12 full days – one for each module – which significantly reduced both cost and administration.

The main change, however, was the launch of a companion Website. This is not only a way for learners, tutors and course administrators to communicate between workshops; it also allows tutors to post articles, exercises and projects for delegates to complete online. Learners can carry out background research and access topical information as well.

Pace and environment were the two key variables. As Lesley Partridge, head of the Worldwide Learning design team, explains: "Reinforcement and retention activities, such as role play, will always be most effective in an interactive workshop session, but our overriding concern was to achieve the correct mix of tone, pace and environment to engage both the hearts and minds. We also wanted to give these learners greater power, to force them to reflect and learn more on the job, whilst giving them the support they needed."

However, tutors on the program stress that the e-facilitation skills required to generate the same learning as a conventional workshop are both considerable and distinct from those used in face to face work. These include running trial sessions to ensure that the learners can use the technology, encouraging informal exchanges over the Website between participants in between formal assignments and ensuring assignments are designed in such a way to encourage maximum two-way communication rather than passive acceptance of a standard line.

KEY LEARNING POINTS

» E-technology has reduced the cost, improved the accessibility and increased the quality of management development initiatives.

» However, the full benefits of e-technology have yet to be realized. Truly personal and collaborative learning using the Internet is now possible but often not achieved either because the organization lacks the necessary software or because its management systems have not caught up.

» Experimentation with the possibilities of new learning technology is also being hampered by the contrasting comfort employees from different backgrounds or with different training have with the technology.

» The key issue currently is whether the personal and collaborative learning involved in fulfilling individual or collective assignments over the Net is possible without the participants having met and "bonded" face to face.

» The consensus among expert trainers is that this face to face contact is necessary. In what is now termed "blended learning," inspirational teaching and ice-breaking groundwork between participants paves the way for follow through assignments and reviews at a distance.

» The sense of intimacy people feel in routine contact and daily work over the Net is changing fast. The balance of the "blend" is therefore constantly under review. A important and growing factor in determining the mix is the skill and creativity of a new breed of trainer, the e-moderator (see News International).

The Global Dimension

» Deng and devolution
» Running before walking
» Plus ça change
» Case study: Volkswagen and Skoda

Before 1989, global management development existed. But it wasn't called that. It was called expatriate training. The dramatic world events of the last 15 years have created a whole new branch of HR strategy and resourcing and in the process a new training function. This is explored in greater depth in the ExpressExec title in the module *Global Training and Development* but a summary of the most important concepts and good practice is provided below.

DENG AND DEVOLUTION

Two events, in particular, triggered globalism in the sense we know it today. The Velvet Revolution in 1989 opened up new markets in first Central and then, following the collapse of the Communist system in Russia in 1994, Eastern Europe; and the culmination of the economic liberalization in China under the reforming party secretary Deng Xiao Ping in his lightning tour of the southern provinces in 1992, which gave the green light to the Pearl River Delta becoming the gateway to trade with the West and ushered in a five-year boom in Hong Kong unprecedented in its history.

Thereafter events flowed with extraordinary rapidity. India, backed by the World Bank and the Asian Development Bank, launched its own privatization program from 1991. Vietnam, shaking off the legacy of a 20-year stand off with the United States, negotiated the lifting of Western trade restrictions in 1995; while Spain, drawing on its own historical provenance, launched a concerted drive to win more markets in Latin America. In Pacific Asia, Singapore and a resurgent Shanghai increasingly challenged Hong Kong's position as the premier trade hub. In a paced series of reforms, markets on mainland China were first liberalized on the Northern coastland and then, in the late 1990s, in the central province of Sichuan.

Management development was caught decidedly off-guard. Expatriate assignments had changed in the 1980s from being the exclusive reserve of "lifers," old hands who stayed in post for the duration only to move to another foreign office, to short-term career postings for promising young talent. However, in accordance with the high-flying nature of management development strategies (see Chapter 3), the numbers were limited and the investment of time by HR specialists in managing the assignment was disproportionately generous in comparison to the rest of the workforce.

The German electronics giant Bosch, for example, considered overseas postings as the perfect training ground for general managers, providing the opportunity for improving linguistic ability, teaching flexibility, generating an international perspective and encouraging a self-starting working style.

Of the 250 expatriates Bosch employed in 1988, less than a tenth were third country nationals and all were recruited internally. Because of this, the company did not use personal inventories to check for key characteristics like flexibility, adaptability and a stable personality. The employee was almost invariably a known quantity already. Expatriates were looked after by the local personnel department and no centrally coordinated mentor system existed.

This was fairly typical of the approach before the world events of the turn of the decade intervened. Fiat was almost unique among the big corporates in the 1980s in analyzing the strengths and weaknesses of its entire management workforce in an international context and in developing a strategy needed for radical improvement. "Selective development" and "growing one's own timber" were the order of the day.

RUNNING BEFORE WALKING

Within five years this strategy had been turned upside down. Expansion into the emerging markets was on a scale never before envisaged and at very short notice. The marketing strategy of the multinationals moved very quickly from exporting or manufacturing locally products or services developed at home by a homogenous board to working with locally recruited managers or suppliers to develop adapted products for a rapidly developing and aspirant local consumer class or business community.

Under the influence of theorists like Christopher Bartlett and Sumantra Goshall, who argued in 1995 that companies were pushed simultaneously towards both global integration and local responsiveness, the phrase "think global, act local" became the new business mantra (see the ExpressExec guide *Global Training and Development*).

Multinational foods and drinks companies like International Distillers built up global brands like Smirnoff vodka but offset the long-term investment in these by developing new spirit blends, such as Black Label whisky, targeted at particular countries like Japan or China. In China, one of the few countries in the world where English has not become the universal business language, Hewlett Packard developed Chinese-language word processing and publishing systems in conjunction with local suppliers like Beijing's Founder Group; while in Mexico, where 70% of its customers are first-time bank users, the Spanish banking group Bilbao y Viscaya tempts prospective investors to make long-term investments by offering them the chance to win prizes.

The old elitist approach to international management development may have helped users to think global, but it did very little to enable them to act local. A number of issues immediately arose which are still being grappled with today and are therefore worth examining in depth.

Building a pool of regional expatriates

The first implication was a dramatically increased need for regional (previously termed "third world") expatriates. Companies found very quickly that targeting and understanding the needs of an increasingly affluent mass market was better undertaken by managers recruited and developed locally and then circulated around the region than outsiders, however authentic their lingual skills and regional or local knowledge.

What this means in practice was spelt out in a survey of 100 multinationals based in Asia by the Economist Intelligence Unit in conjunction with the Wyatt Company in 1994. The report confirmed the rising presence of locally recruited expatriates. In the previous five years, locally recruited expatriates were forecast to increase by two-thirds while overseas postings filled by North Americans or Europeans had dropped by a fifth.

However, the survey also vividly portrayed the scale of the training and career management challenge this presented. Three-quarters of expatriates employed by the sample were on their first assignment and the speed and scale with which locally recruited expatriates were being assigned was bankrupting the resources of regional or local HR expertise to provide them with effective induction or preparation – a failing exacerbated by the fact that until then many companies, Western and Asian alike, saw locally recruited expatriates as an attraction because they were cheaper to employ.

In fact, the induction and preparation required by locally recruited expatriates was significantly higher than that conventionally provided to their North American and European counterparts. Contrary to the rather naïve assumptions made by Western executives, expatriates from one part of the region were more likely to encounter racism and hostility from local staff in another than if they were "white."

Early expectations that new mainland Chinese operations could be resourced by Hong Kong nationals, for example, were dashed when it became clear that discrimination against Cantonese-speaking Southerners everywhere other than their homelands was intense – and that the hostility was enthusiastically reciprocated. The same applied to Malaysian and Singaporean recruits, even if they were recruited from long-standing Chinese diaspora communities.

In addition, Asian managers generally were more reluctant to take up expatriate postings for a whole host of reasons that included a lack of appropriate schooling and cultural facilities, more extensive extended family responsibilities and a widely held perception, reinforced by experience, that expatriate postings in Asia were "assignments to oblivion."

The experiences of one highly qualified Indonesian manager, interviewed in the EIU report, illustrates what happened when he was transferred to Hong Kong:

> "I was looking for proper logistics and support when I arrived. I was expecting someone would be delegated to look after me and would be specifically trained to handle the difficult problems I would encounter. In fact, the manager assigned to look after my interests was not trained to look after the needs of third country nationals. He gave me the sense that he was feeling 'You are Indonesian. You shouldn't be here, but since you are I suppose I better give you some help.' There was no dedicated human resource professional to support him and no company guidelines for him to fall back on."

Training and career management was the problem. So it has proved the solution. Well over 60% of the employers in the EIU report now link expatriate assignment to some form of career development in an attempt to build up an international pool of senior managers. Even the trauma of the economic cutbacks throughout the region in the late 1990s and the collapse of the Japanese financial markets has not left the pool stagnant.

Constant reassurance and well-managed moves across the board are, however, the key. Asia-based firms have found that sending junior and middle managers to countries with more advanced economies increases the likelihood that they will be poached if the expatriates are not provided with a convincing impression of what will happen to them after the first assignment.

Martyn Fisher, regional human resource and training director of Deloitte Touche Tohmatsu for much of the 1990s, argues that sophisticated long-term career strategies of the kind once only offered to high flyers, like the two-year professional program offered by his own firm, where formal training is linked to a series of overseas assignments in other practices, is the only way of keeping talented staff in Thailand and Indonesia, where Western professional skills are still in short supply. Like many other consultancies worldwide, Deloitte also recruits more junior consultants than it actually needs in the long term, in expectation that it will lose between a third and a half of the original intake.

Training in modern management methods

Globalism in the early 1990s was launched in the West on the spring-board of a total quality management revolution which had transformed multinational corporations who had previously been – in terms of their hierarchy, bureaucracy and quality standards – very little different from the firms they now encountered in developing countries. The legacy of centralized controlled economies in countries emerging from Communism was also deeply rooted.

A similar process of reform was now initiated by the MNCs covering both newly recruited staff in their own operations and the work-force they inherited through the purchase of local subsidiaries. The process was extended still further by insisting that all local suppliers or consultancies win ISO or equivalent accreditation.

The experiences of General Electric when it acquired the Hungarian light bulb manufacturer Tungsram following the collapse of the

Comecon economy is fairly typical. Under the supervision of production director Don McKenna, time between order and delivery at Tungsram plants was slashed – from 90 days in 1990 to 32 days in 1994. Breakages on the production line were cut over the same period from a staggering one in two in pre-GE days to near world standards.

The true acid test of the reforms, however, lay in GE's ability to promote team work and Western-style project management in a culture previously reliant on rigid demarcation. "Our world totally changed," says project manager Tibor Fricsan, who saw Tungsram's layers of management cut from 11 to three in less than two years. Tamas Palopia, senior leadership technology director, agrees. "People who were used to a hierarchical structure where the boss gave the orders had to adjust in a very short period of time to the idea that decisions are taken by teams and not individuals."

Much of this could have been said by any line manager in North America and Europe during the TQM revolution in the West a few years earlier. However, the fact that Hungary and other Central European countries had only just emerged from 40 years of a command economy added a new twist to the adjustment. Under the socialists, exhortations to greater productivity were seen as political slogans to be ignored or bypassed. The result was that, while GE executives regarded phrases such as "empowerment" and "a culture of winning" as articles of faith, to supervisors and workers on the shop floor they bore a confusing similarity to the slogans of the old order.

"Providing junior managers and supervisors with the necessary team building and project leadership skills was the easy part," says Bob Lubecky, who joined Tungsram in 1992 as director of technology from GE's halogen engineering business in the US. "It was getting over the message that the need to work across boundaries and break down internal barriers were not words you put on a banner or a factory poster and forgot, but things you put into practice in your day to day work, that was the real challenge."

Benchmarking and knowledge transfer

Much of the knowledge and skills transfer in the first wave of globalism was one way. Locally recruited managers, such as Tibor Fricsan and Tamas Palopia at Tungsram, were acting as brokers, gatekeepers and pulsetakers for products, services, and ways of working that had been developed by their employers in another world. The training they received, in common with all other employees, was to conduct business the company way.

But as the "think global, act local" message sank home and corporations started to realize that they would only be able to develop new markets by adapting or re-examining their existing products or services, so the need for genuine organizational learning on a global scale started to take hold.

Unlike the 1980s, when this kind of two-way knowledge transfer was confined to the Board or the senior management team, largely to grafting externally recruited executives to an organically home-grown body, the global benchmarking that took place in the following decade was at all levels.

Global task forces were created to facilitate this exchange. In 1994, for example, the international branded foods and drink giant Grand Metropolitan (subsequently merged into the Diageo group) assembled its top marketing, finance, human resources and general managers in a program called "Spearhead China."

Although the group invited in top experts on doing business in mainland China to advise them, the real focus of the program was to gather and, on a group-wide basis, profit from the rich mine of internal expertise and data that had previously been jealously hoarded by operating companies. Among the group were managers with over 20 years of experience of Asian operations and no attempt had been made to tap their knowledge.

Similarly, a cardinal aim of the in-company MBA program launched by Standard Chartered Bank in conjunction with the UK's Henley Management College (see previous chapter) was to use projects and assignments conducted under the program by managers as far afield as Tokyo, Singapore, Harare and Sidcup was to share good practice and new insights into the company's disparate markets.

One enormous benefit was a wholly new approach to customer service. Standard Chartered's activities in North America and Europe was largely confined to project and corporate finance. In developing countries in Africa and Asia, it operates retail and high street banking. In pre-1997 Hong Kong, for example, it was one of two banks printing the local currency. Largely as a consequence of the international interaction generated by the MBA program, Standard Chartered's operations in the West realized that it had more to learn from its own internal customer services practices in Asia than it did from other banking competitors.

Cross-company alliances and consortia

The need for knowledge transfer and exchange has reached new heights with the creation of sophisticated strategic alliances. The German airline Lufthansa, for example, played a leading role in setting up the Star Alliance in 1995, comprising America's United Airlines, Scandinavian Airlines (SAS), Varig (of Brazil), Air Canada and Thai.

At the time, Star was easily the largest alliance of its kind in terms of the number of companies involved. Unusually, there was no central authority. In terms of "soft" issues like customer service and relationship marketing, the strength of the network depended then and still does today on its weakest link. There was no obvious mechanism for the stronger members like Lufthansa to exert pressure on the weaker airlines. Any improvement had to be achieved through sharing experience and best practice.

With this in mind, HR director Thomas Sattelberger designed a series of programs and events intended not only to instill an "Alliance mentality" among staff from different members of the Star conglomerate, but to encourage them to share their knowledge and experience. These included roadshows to communicate the ideas and vision of the Alliance, cross-cultural workshops, and joint management development programs designed specifically to encourage upcoming executives from the member companies to work together in developing new strategies for the Alliance.

This kind of cross-boundary exchange and synergy is something only the largest corporate alliances are able to undertake using their own resources and expertise. Consortium programs, usually run in conjunction with an international business school, have been the more common resort.

The global consortium program launched by London Business School in 1995 is a good example. This brings together such companies as ABB, Lufthansa, Standard Chartered Bank and SFK to help develop a generation of senior managers capable of leading their organization into the next phase of global development. In common with the current emphasis on benchmarking and cross-boundary learning, the emphasis is on participants learning from each other, comparing the way their respective organizations manage complex businesses, expand their presence in emerging markets and manage across borders.

Each module, attended by six managers nominated by each member company, starts with a session on the creation and delivery of global strategy, covering issues such as effective joint-venture management and global people management. It then focuses on how consortium companies should manage their response to local issues and developments through face to face discussions with leading politicians, academics and front line managers from Asia, South America and Europe. The last session in each module helps companies explore how they can incorporate the new ideas and issues into their long-term strategy.

This "curriculum" is supported by a number of exercises designed to reinforce the team-based approach to learning. Company teams prepare an analysis of their own organization and present it during the first module. Cross-company teams are assigned an organization to focus on and have the opportunity for an in-depth discussion with the chief executive during the last module. Two days of each module are spent examining how specific consortium members have created a competitive advantage in one region of the world.

In 1998, for example, managers from Standard Chartered Bank described how it built up its banking operations in Asia; managers from SFK reported on its manufacturing strategy in São Paulo; managers from British Telecom discussed its strategy for entry into global markets; and managers from Lufthansa reported on its alliance with the Brazilian airline Varig.

As a way of helping participants incorporate what they have learned on the program into their own work, the tutors issue a "CEO challenge." This forms the basis for work by participants from the same company throughout the program and culminates in a presentation to their own chief executive.

In 1998, Standard Chartered Bank's six managers were given the task of understanding the Japanese market; SFK's managers were asked to build a second brand for the company; BT's managers were asked to present proposals for how their company could develop a more effective alliance structure; and Lufthansa's managers were asked to develop a strategy for the next stage of the company's ambitious Star Alliance (see above).

With 36 managers having taken part each year since its inception, the program has many former participants, who are now being tapped as a further source of learning and support. The program has also developed its own dedicated source of training materials.

"We change the content each year to fit in with the developments in each company and the rather dramatic changes in the commercial environment in which they operate," says program director Professor Lynda Gratton. "But what makes the learning so effective is our ability to relate this to the case presentations made by the participants themselves. We have now started to take this material and write it up as formal case studies for future use on the program."

PLUS ÇA CHANGE

In summary, the key to effective global management development has been more a matter of efficient logistics than a design imposed uniquely by the international nature of the exercise.

Early teambuilding and project management skills were introduced in developing countries in the 1990s using almost identical methods to those used in the West during the previous decade. The barriers encountered were determined less by any deeply ingrained cultural forces – respect for elders and the paramount position of the family were, after all, hallmarks of North America and Europe in the 1950s and the counter-culture of young people in Asia and Central Europe in the 1990s very similar to that of the West 20 years before – but rather the rigid demarcations of traditional organizational hierarchy.

A survey of 60 multinationals operating throughout Asia in 1995 by Hong Kong's Poon Kam Kai Institute of Management found that their experiences in introducing modern management skills in the region was almost identical to those in their home country, in terms of the response of local managers and supervisors. There was a slightly greater resistance to flatter, devolved styles of working but these were the by-product of a unreformed top-down management culture and not necessarily deeply rooted social *mores*. Enterprises in operation in "post-Communist" economies found they faced a bigger challenge in shifting ideas and attitudes but, ironically, the barriers – principally, an unwillingness to experiment and take the initiative without authorization from above – were little different from that of a "vertical" firm operating in a non-socialist country.

Only in the key area of relationship building and networking have cross-cultural skills been more important than they would have been at home. Moreover, the skills in question – good lingual ability, sensitivity and affinity with contrasting social customs and a knowledge and appreciation of the country's or region's history and how this has shaped attitudes to business or trade – have little to do with conventional management training and more with personal experiences and education obtained outside the workplace.

Rather it has been the challenge of freeing up the time and resources to bring together managers from different locations and availabilities to engage in the kind of intense learning and exchange required by modern management programs that has most taxed senior HR practitioners. The development of sophisticated intranet software and discussion databases has made the task easier (see previous chapter); but so long as it is felt that bringing people together in a single room is essential to team building and organizational learning, the challenge will remain.

As the program director for GrandMet's 1994 Spearhead China program commented: "Coming up with the design is the easy part. It is getting the commitment that takes the time."

CASE STUDY: VOLKSWAGEN AND SKODA

A template example of the challenges facing global companies is the German automobile giant Volkswagen's decision to put management development at the heart of its efforts to forge a viable alliance with its Czech counterpart Skoda. At the time the joint venture was launched in April 1991, Skoda was regarded as a sick joke by many Western car manufacturers; but as Skoda's Biagio Morabito stresses, in the eyes of its managers and by the (flawed) standards of the region, Skoda was one of the top producers of Central Europe and a company which they were proud to work for.

"Before the revolution of 1989, Skoda was an exemplary state enterprise," he stresses. "All the main decisions of the enterprise were subject to state planning. Quantitative achievement of planned figures took absolute priority over entrepreneurial decisions. The organization of the company corresponded to socialist structure, being centralistic and autocratic.

"Accordingly, management composed of a director and his seven deputies was strictly hierarchical. Purchasing and selling prices were not subject to the laws of offer and demand, but were controlled by government. In addition, investment and production volumes were subject to state planning. However, Skoda was able to organize its production and work processes itself. A great production depth and high level of supplies were designed to make the enterprise independent."

Looking back in the light of what he knows now about the West's production techniques, Skoda, compared with other East European automobile manufacturers, was to Morabito "the one-eyed king in the country of the blind;" by East European standards, a good company which, however, was incapable of withstanding international competition.

In these circumstances, Skoda as a potential partner for a Western car manufacturer offered a number of strengths and a number of weaknesses. The morale of its managers and workers was high. In its own eyes, Skoda, one of the oldest automobile manufacturers in Europe, had a long tradition of success in its traditional markets such as the countries of the former Soviet Union and Poland, and a trade mark to be proud of. It still had the pioneering spirit that, once again in its own eyes, had developed creative and original solutions to bypass the constraints of a politically motivated command economy. And, in common with most other East European enterprises, it had a well-qualified workforce in engineering and quantitative management techniques, although little or no understanding of customer service and market research.

The challenge for Volkswagen was to introduce new production techniques that would make the company capable of competing in new international markets without undermining the sense of pride that Skoda's managers and workers had in their company.

At a time when leading German car firms like BMW and Volkswagen were themselves facing increasing pressure from Japanese and US competition, this was no easy task. As Peter Kunz, the human resources director responsible for designing the process of learning explains:

> "Volkswagen was passing through its own change process. Our technical knowledge was high but our ability to respond to change has been slower. We therefore felt that simply introducing our own proven methods of the past would not be enough. Skoda would be lagging behind VW and would be one step behind us and could never arrive at international competitors' level.
>
> "In addition, a direct carry-over of knowledge would have totally ignored the origin and present-day state of Skoda in the Czech Republic, and even ignore or destroy the fruitful starting points of the past. Possibly, considerable passive resistance of the local workers defending their own cultural identity would result."

The solution VW came up with was a strategy of "know-how transfer" that would enable Skoda managers to link their own traditions with modern VW approaches to international competition. The strategy took the form of a four-part process.

1 At the start of the joint venture, managers from the Volkswagen group were appointed into key positions at Skoda such as sales, controlling and quality management. Through these managers, the basic strategy of Skoda was agreed with VW Group management.
2 Other principal functions were filled, on a shared basis, by a local Skoda manager and a VW expatriate. The German manager acted as a "buddy," teaching and coaching the Czech manager. As the local manager gained confidence and increasingly took over responsibility, the expatriate drew back from operative and strategic tasks and concentrated solely on coaching. As Peter Kunz explains, the demands on the coach are high. "If their social ability is insufficient there is a danger that his or her Czech colleague will become incapable of taking action due to a state of insecurity, and will take over the role of a mere assistant to the German partner – not our intention at all."

3 Counselors and specialists supported the Czech colleague on site for a period of up to one year in fields of activity where up-to-date specific know-how was lacking.

4 In some fields, for example personnel management, the transfer of know-how took place through project management. The Czech manager in this case is the only holder of the function and is thus secure in his status and activity. Together with German counterparts in VW, these Czech managers define a series of projects directly linked to the joint venture strategy in which they cooperate and, in the course of time, take control of.

As Kunz stresses, the demands this placed on the German manager-buddies acting as coaches and tutors was immense. VW has built up a series of competencies that they regard as essential if the relationship with their Czech counterparts is to succeed (see box below).

These include: *intercultural sensitivity and open-mindedness*, including a readiness to live in the Czech Republic and to try to understand the country and the people; *leadership and the ability to change roles*, in particular the ability to change over between a patriarchal and partner-like style of management and the confidence to "let go" and make oneself superfluous; *process competence*, being able to identify the most important tasks, converting these into processes with measurable results; and *the ability of analysis and learning*, being able to ask the right questions and link aspects of the local environment with one's own know-how.

Finally, and perhaps most importantly, there was what Kunz refers to as "standing," the ability to link the positive aspects of the two corporate cultures – that of the Czech environment and one's own Volkswagen culture, and reflect both of these perspectives of business in a self-confident manner.

These competencies were developed as a result of hard experience. Among the many mistakes VW and Skoda made and rectified during the early years are choosing engineering specialists to perform the roles that should have been undertaken by experienced managers with interpersonal skills; failing to provide any individual preparation for the role of coach and recipient of the learning, with the result that the two parties only try to deal with the solution of production problems, not the process of learning; failing to define the role tightly enough, with the result that some German managers feel solely responsible for strategy development and report to VW Group management, leaving the Czech manager with only operative tasks; and failing to provide any systematic and rapid process of informing staff about changes in strategy in a fast moving industry, with the result that Germans wind up talking to Germans and not Czechs.

However, Skoda's Biagio Morabito is a firm believer in the theories of "double loop" learning pioneered by Harvard Business School's Professor Chris Argyris (see Chapter 8), curiosity is followed by disillusionment which in turns leads to perseverance and ultimately success.

"With Volkswagen support, Skoda is entering the New Age in large steps," he concludes. "After initial euphoria, a phase of sobriety has set in. The process of change is more complicated and lengthy than was originally expected. At present, at a time that is also characterized by difficult overall economic conditions, the main point is to follow up on the fruitful beginnings we created in the first five years consistently and unremittingly. If this is done, success will be certain for us."

COMPETENCIES AT VOLKSWAGEN FOR TRANSFERRING KNOW-HOW TO SKODA MANAGERS

» Intercultural sensitivity and open-mindedness – including the readiness to live in the Czech Republic and to try to understand the country and the people.

» Leadership and the ability to change roles, in particular the ability to change over between a patriarchal and partner-like style of management depending on the situation, and the readiness and confidence to "let go" and make oneself superfluous.

» Process competence, identifying the most important tasks in an organizational unit, converting these to processes with measurable results and placing them in a strategic and forward-looking context.

» Ability of analysis and learning, asking the right questions and purposefully linking usable aspects of the local environment with one's own know-how.

» Standing, having the ability to link the positive aspects of the two corporate cultures – that of the Czech environment and one's own original Volkswagen culture – and reflecting these in one's actions towards both sides in a self-confident manner.

THE 10 MAJOR MISTAKES INITIALLY MADE BY GERMAN AND CZECH MANAGERS IN THE PROCESS OF KNOW-HOW TRANSFER

1 Wrong choice of personnel on both sides – for example, specialists selected instead of experienced managers.

2 No individual preparation for the role of know-how donor and acceptor.

3 The two parties only try to deal with the solution of production problems, not with the process of learning.

4 The German manager feels responsible for strategy development and reports to VW Group management, leaving the Czech manager with only operative tasks.

5 No systematic and rapid process of informing staff about all the principal changes – in critical situations the Germans only talk to Germans.

6 The expatriate is concerned with his profile and status, while the Czech managers appear satisfied with the role of "assistant."

7 At the start, the expatriate fails to set up a list of the existing processes that work but immediately questions everything, pushing through his own concepts and as a result "de-skilling" the Czech managers.

8 The entire organization is too task-oriented, with little attempt made to gain cooperation through team building and regular briefings with Czech managers.

9 There are no unambiguous agreements as to strategic and management targets.

10 There is no joint self-critical reflection as to milestones in the development of the new organizational unit.

Source: Peter Kunz, Human Resources/ZPK SKODA, automobilova a.s.

KEY LEARNING POINTS

» Global management strategies have moved, very fast, from being an ancillary to the recruitment and transfer of expatriates to the principal means of achieving commonly held standards and values which are seamless and easily transferable across geographical boundaries.

» In the early years of globalism, when establishing common quality standards was a priority, the process was a top-down affair, established through "cascading" workshops and seminars that established a consensus in one layer of management before moving onto the next (lower) one.

» Now the dynamic is becoming more bottom up and sideways. The diverse views held by a global workforce made up of people with different or locally informed perspectives of both the business and its markets are being tapped through seminars that act as think tanks and brainstorms. Learning through social serendipity rather than codified rules is the main goal.

The State of the Art

» Linking development to strategy
» Testing assumptions
» Design: Cause and effect
» Choosing and briefing a supplier

What immediately becomes apparent when you examine the trends outlined in the previous chapters is that there is no quick fix to effective management development. The overriding lesson from the demise of old style fast track strategies is that no matter how thorough the work undertaken in researching what is needed at the start of the exercise, unforeseen events will overturn three-quarters of the assumptions made within a matter of a few years. Unless the process is subject to constant review and adjustment, a homogenous management team will result, capable only of dealing with yesterday's problems.

When looking at state of the art practice, then, any discussion about the practicalities of implementing a management development strategy needs to be preceded by what measures are in place to link the strategy to the organization's key activities and plans.

LINKING DEVELOPMENT TO STRATEGY

In the wake of the radical changes to business and society that threatened to overwhelm organizations in the late 1980s and early 1990s, commentators like McGill University's Henry Minzberg and London Business School's Gary Hamel claimed that strategy as the world then understood it was dead.

By this they did not mean that it was useless for senior executives to make plans for the future. Far from it. They meant that the old way of doing it, based on financial projections by department heads underpinned by performance targets spread over a 1–5 year period, was useless in a world where market changes were occurring week by week and month by month.

In the new world order, the challenge was having the right talent in place to meet needs that were difficult to predict by analytical or mathematical projections. A number of ways of identifying the future management needs of organizations have been tried and these are well summarized by Chris Hayes and Nickie Fonda, authors of *Competence and Competition* (see Chapter 8).

» *The scenario*: The environment of the organization in 5, 10 or 25 years is sketched out. From this, pressures on the firm are deduced, and conclusions are drawn about the company's future management needs.

» *Critical success factors*: Key aspects of the overall business philosophy and strategy over the next few years are made explicit (often issued in the form of a "mission statement"). Key performance indicators for the strategy are also identified. These are translated into critical contributions expected from managers and then into managerial attributes.

» *The human resources approach*: Companies with a long track record of successful performance for the attributes of their managers which have contributed to their success. Commonly occurring attributes are identified and imported. The common use of benchmarking, consortia and learning alliances between like-minded organizations (see Chapter 7) have made this task easier.

» *The learning needs approach*: The environment is scanned for a potential future medium-term demand on managers, for instance the use of virtual working or e-communications. Other organizations' experience is drawn on to devise a role description for effective management performance. From this description, managerial attributes and competencies are deduced.

» *The strategic competence assessment*: The performance of units and departments is reviewed not only in terms of performance against plans and targets, but also in relation to the business strategy and the strengths and weaknesses it has shown in dealing with the unanticipated. Development needs for managers in that part of the business are then deduced.

The advantage of all of these approaches, Hayes and Fonda stress, is that they attempt to "position" a company's managers to cope with its environment. They are therefore not limited to a short-term financial projection of the likely position in a year or two. Their weakness is that they are heavily dependent on the quality of the conclusions that are drawn and that these are unlikely to be definitive. New and anticipated needs generally emerge over time. Even though they look to the medium to longer term, they must be reviewed frequently.

Example: The Hong Kong government 1992–97

Few organizations undergo the changes experienced by the Hong Kong government in the mid-1990s. Faced with an impending transfer of sovereignty from the UK to China, government departments were also under pressure to live up to the consequences of their early success.

Many civil servants had been recruited into the territory's government in the 1950s when the main priority, in the light of the influx of refugees from Shanghai and other cities recently taken over by the Communists, was to provide basic food and shelter for a burgeoning population.

Little changed as Hong Kong developed as a trade entrepot in the 1960s and 1970s. But its transformation into an international financial center by the late 1980s, partly because of the opening up of China's coastal districts, created a population with higher expectations of a government which, in a virtual city state, acted both as a local authority and a national executive.

A number of government departments suffered intense pressure. The urban services department faced increased demands from a prosperous middle class for better sports and leisure amenities. A nascent awareness of environmental issues resulted in a "greening of Hong Kong" campaign, involving the planting of 10,000 trees as well as the creation of a large municipal park at the heart of the city. Lax health and safety regulations were subject to intense scrutiny following a number of minor typhoid epidemics, when water used to store fish in Hong Kong's popular Lamma Island restaurants was found to have been drawn from bays adjacent to sewage outlets.

The geo-technical department, in transition from being staffed by expatriates to being staffed by local managers, had to deal with the consequences of growing business developments and housing estates on mountainous territory that was prone to landslides. In 1994 a mudslide at the busy port of Aberdeen, in which nine people were killed and 20 injured, resulted in the government taking most of the blame, despite (or because of) a tactless public relations campaign pointing out that slope safety was the responsibility of individual land owners. Though this was true in law, it looked like government buck passing.

The labor department was caught unawares by the onset of a recession in 1995 in a city that took full employment for granted. It was obliged at very short notice to set up Western-style retraining and job-seeking services without any experience in how they should be run. This was made politically more complex by the influx of large numbers of semi-skilled workers from the mainland, taking advantage of the relaxations in labor mobility regulations introduced by Deng Xiaoping's reforms.

Then there were the pressures of Hong Kong's status in the world. An influx of foreign companies keen to use Hong Kong as a base for expansion into the special economic territories on the mainland set up by China's reforms created a new political constituency, capable of exerting significant pressure on the government on local issues as well as matters of international trade.

An example was the friction between the meteorological office and the business community over typhoon warnings during Hong Kong's stormy autumn. When a Typhoon 8 warning (which requires all schools to be closed and all workers to return home) was issued in 1994 and the typhoon failed to materialize, the business community complained bitterly about the lost revenue. A month later the office failed to issue a full typhoon warning and one did materialize, so the government came under attack for risking lives.

Lastly, there were the political reforms introduced by the last UK governor Chris Patten which, although watered down by the incoming Chinese administration, helped to create an expectation of local accountability that had never previously existed, even under British rule. A new directly elected legislative assembly coincided with the launch of new newspapers, business cable channels and local Chinese-speaking radio and television companies, imposing an obligation on civil servants to present and explain public policy in a way for which they had been prepared.

To meet these new pressures and demands, the government launched a campaign called "Serving the Community," covering the 85 branches of the civil service employing 180,000 staff. The campaign was dedicated to meeting four publicly stated guiding principles that would govern everything the government did. The wording below is the one adopted in the launch of the initiative in the Legislative Assembly.

» *Being accountable*: Because government has an obligation to answer to the community which it exists to serve.
» *Living within our means*: Because the government determines how best to meet the community's needs within the resources available.

» *Managing for performance*: Because the community rightly expects the government to deliver the best possible services for public money.
» *Developing a culture of service*: Because government services are delivered to individuals who rightly expect to be treated fairly and decently.

VALUES ARISING FROM THE GUIDING PRINCIPLES

» Leadership
» Openness
» Expertise
» Effectiveness
» Commitment
» Integrity
» Courtesy
» Responsiveness
» Partnership
» Foresight
» Propriety
» Efficiency

Source: Hong Kong Civil Service, 1995.

Following the "Critical Success Factors" framework set out above, the guiding principles were designed to act as the inspiration for a series of management values that would underpin the work of all civil servants and contractors working for the government (see box above).

These in turn would be defined in such a way to act as springboard for a series of management development initiatives designed to provide individuals with the skills and qualities they needed to uphold the principles in their day to day work.

Drawing on international best practice, the Hong Civil Service Training Department translated the values into a series of change management competencies that could be used as the basis for all future training initiatives. These included the following, the wording once again being that used in government documents.

» *Foresight*. Managing change means being able to take charge, not being inhibited by old ways of thinking and being willing to champion and try out original ideas, new procedures and new ways of doing things. These may be difficult to understand and even threatening to some people. Effective managers need to challenge outdated ideas and processes without alienating or undermining people who still believe in them.

» *Leadership*. Leading people through change involves helping them to see the vision and direction of the organization, working towards clear objectives and finding ways to help them add value to and improve the services they provide to internal or external customers. Having sought new ideas and selected the ones that might work, effective managers must convince large numbers of people that they are worth investing in and implementing.

» *Partnership*. Change does not occur on its own. It can only happen when people who share the same views and ideas seek out each other and act together. Managers cannot work effectively if they hide behind their specialist functions.

» *Communication*. The presentation of new ideas and policies must make them relate to the work of front-line staff and not seem part of a grand design in which employees are not involved. Effective managers present change using vocabulary and analogies that make sense to the people who will be most affected by it.

» *Openness and responsiveness*. Just as effective managers need to challenge outdated concepts, so they need to be open to the new ideas of others. In periods of rapid change it helps to be a listener, an observer and a monitor. In its broadest sense, being open to new information and ideas means being able to set aside your own preconceptions and accept other points of view.

Lingua franca , not *lingua forte*

So far, so good. But what does "being open to new ideas" and "not hiding behind specialist functions" mean in the context of a

Hong Kong civil servant's day to day work? And how will individuals' preconceptions about the role of managers in the organization either color the way they interpret the role or prompt them to discriminate between one role and another? In her study *What Makes a Manager?* (see Chapter 8) Dr Wendy Hirsh makes the following assertion:

> "Managers draw on the way key skills are described all over the organization to take decisions about themselves and their subordinates. As skill descriptions have to be short and simple, it is hardly surprising that major employers tend to look for the same sort of qualities and skills. Everyone is hunting for the bright, keen, innovative communicators who can make good decisions and .take their staff with them. However, the recruitment and career decisions based on these descriptions only achieve an acceptable degree of consistency if all managers thoroughly understand and share their real meaning."

A worldwide study of the role of senior managers by Professor Andrew Kakabadse of the UK's Cranfield School of Management, involving 2,500 people in Europe and 1,400 in Asia, found significant differences in the quality of dialogue and common purpose respondents enjoyed with their colleagues and subordinates.

In Japan, for example, sensitive issues tend not to be raised because to do so would generate unacceptable levels of discomfort among certain members of the team. In some cases, senior managers knowingly allow the organization to deteriorate rather than openly facing up to the problem. In these circumstances, competency frameworks which exhort managers to "challenge outdated ideas and processes" or "convince large numbers of people that they [workable innovations] are worth investing in" need to focus specific resources on helping teams engage in open and honest discussions.

In China, the Cranfield study found the barriers less due to an inability to share information and views and more because people, in the words of the HKCVTD competency framework, "hide behind their specialist functions." Chinese managers, compared with a cross-section of their European counterparts, felt most comfortable working to clear demarcations of right and wrong behavior and identified more closely with the status conferred on them by their professional qualification than by their role as managers.

As a consequence, much of the most important training work undertaken by the civil service in the wake of the "Serving the Community" initiative was in joint scenario planning and crisis management exercises that helped different departments plan and implement joint initiatives like the "greening of Hong Kong" campaign.

Of course cultural differences are not determined only by nationality. Dr Wendy Hirsh's research on skills descriptions (see above) found that even within one sector in the UK – financial services – the interpretations of common management functions varied with (and even within) company culture and with the specific job role of the manager. Good decision making in one company means taking innovative decisions. In another it means analyzing hard data and minimizing commercial risk.

Her conclusions are set out in more detail in Chapter 8, Key Concepts and Thinkers.

TESTING ASSUMPTIONS

For all these reasons, however thorough the upfront analysis of management skills, investment in any management development activity needs to be preceded by both *organizational needs analysis* (ONA) to test the strategic assumptions underpinning the initiative; and *training needs analysis* (TNA) to check whether the expectations and assumptions of the participants are compatible with the aims of the program.

In part, good training needs analysis acts as a guard against the organization and the individual acting or thinking with cross-purpose; and that the resources available are sufficient to meet the challenge.

The Hong Kong Civil Service change management program (see above), for example, encouraged individuals to work with their managers to develop the skills and qualities they felt they lacked or were unsure of. The process was underpinned by a guide to self-development that took the competencies outlined in the "Values" box above and enabled individuals to pinpoint the ones that applied most to their own jobs.

This strategy presupposed that individual civil servants were happy to admit to their weaknesses; that their managers had been provided with the training and coaching skills to respond; and that the training facilities in place were flexible enough to meet the increased and more complex demands made on them.

In fact, TNA exercises carried out two years into the initiatives revealed that most staff disliked getting feedback on their performance; that most line managers disliked giving it; and that, with the exception of the urban services department, which boasts its own training center, appraisal and training facilities were insufficient to support the necessary culture change. Furthermore, the impetus behind the initiative – very much that of the governor Chris Patten – was being progressively undermined as there was no certainty whether the reforms would continue beyond the handover of the territory to China in 1997.

TNA and ONA exercises are also essential because they highlight whether the analysis of the problem or challenge, nearly always undertaken by senior managers or HR practitioners, is accurate. Two recent consultancy assignments carried out by the authors illustrate the contrast between perception and reality.

Example 1: International law firm

An international law firm conducted market research that suggested that while their principal clients were happy with the services provided by partners, they felt the performance of junior and senior associates was lacking.

As part of a larger partner training initiative, a seminar was planned to focus on the delegation skills of partners in respect of their associate staff (termed fee earners). To better inform the design and the briefing of tutors and contributors, a structured interview was conducted with a selection of partners of different ages and experience and from different practices within the firm (see box below). Their feedback was then compared with the responses of a selection of fee earners, again of varying levels of experience and seniority, from the same practices.

The results (see second box below) suggested that poor delegation skills, which undoubtedly existed, were part of a much bigger picture. Fee earners' performance was not only being undermined by inconsistent and idiosyncratic briefing and supervision techniques, but also by the fact that they were receiving little or no career management support. Partners adopted a "sink or swim" approach and there was no obligation, or techniques available, to "bring on" poor performers.

Poor human resource management resulted, with successful fee earners being loaded with more and more as poor performers were abandoned by the wayside.

Drawing on the feedback, the tutors designed a scenario exercise where partners were obliged to engage in sophisticated project management and team-based exercises, selecting and monitoring the performance of a number of fee earners working collectively on a large international case. Had the tutors relied on the briefing provided by the senior partners, the session would have focused solely on one-to-one delegation skills.

STRUCTURED INTERVIEW (INTERNATIONAL LAW FIRM)

This interview allows us to assess more accurately your own personal development needs and also to position any formal training in the context of the work processes and relationships that exist in the firm. All information provided will remain strictly confidential.

1 What role do you play in the firm? Which are your areas of legal expertise? Which industries or sectors do you have closest knowledge of?
2 Where do you think the firm is strong in the service it provides to its clients? Where do you think it could be stronger?
3 Without breaching any confidentiality obligations (or naming the client), give us examples of 2–3 client "matters" that you have supervised in the last six months.
4 What support have you required from fee earners in effectively handling these matters? Where, in your opinion, has this support been most effectively provided? Where, in your opinion, has it been weakest?
5 How much routine contact do you have with fee earners who support you in client matters? Do you have daily contact with them on business issues? Do you have any routine social contact with them?

6 What, in your opinion, are the measures most likely to motivate the fee earners who support you in dealing with client matters?

7 To what extent are you directly involved in HR issues directly connected with the development of fee earners who support you in dealing with client matters [such as reward, training, performance appraisal, promotion and personal or professional counseling]?

8 How long do administrative staff expect to work for the firm? What, in your opinion, are the measures most likely to aid in their retention?

9 Do you prefer to operate within clearly delineated roles and responsibilities, where actions and procedures are agreed to and assessed against highly visible and quantitative measures of performance? Or do you prefer to operate within a looser framework, where the desired outcome is agreed in advance but the method used to reach that outcome is left to the individual to whom it is delegated? What constraints on your management style are imposed by issues of client confidentiality and legal probate?

10 Finally, how do you rate yourself in terms of supervision and delegation and on what specific areas would you like to focus your personal development in this area?

Thank you. We will use the feedback you have provided to focus our efforts more accurately on the real needs of partners. The specific needs we cannot deal with in the formal session will be followed up through an e-mail bulletin.

TRAINING NEEDS ANALYSIS (INTERNATIONAL LAW FIRM)

The following assumptions and related issues about the development needs of partners at the firm are based on the feedback we received from the six partners and four fee earners.

Assumptions

» Attitudes and practice in the field of supervision and delegation at the firm is dominated, not surprisingly, by traditions that have grown up in the management practice. The administrative structures adopted by the practice have very little influence on management styles, which tend to be driven by the individual preferences, experience and (occasionally) prejudices of each individual partner. Given the flexible allocation of resources to each client matter, with fee earners allocated according to need, good (and bad) practice in each project depends on the preferred style of the matter partner and his or her assessment of the dependability of the assistant.

» Supervision and delegation in the management practice are also shaped by the nature of the marketplace. A high proportion of the work is legally contentious, leaving little scope for pardonable error. Clients in this sector expect to deal directly with the matter partner in all but the most trivial issues and appear willing to pay premium fees for the privilege. By contrast matters in other sectors, such as property and I&T, involve a far higher proportion of non-contentious legal work and clients who are prepared to respond to matter partners' arguments that they will gain better value by dealing regularly on less important issues with reliable fee earners who are charged out at a lower cost.

» Consequently most partners in the management practice are more reluctant to follow the practice of their colleagues in other sectors in delegating discrete areas of work to tried and trusted fee earners. Some may be happy to give selected assistants the responsibility of sending out a proportion of key correspondence on their own initiative – under a partner's or their own name. Others insist on seeing everything, sometimes re-working large chunks of it.

» This can be exacerbated by a culture of excellence and client service among partners which is not generally underpinned by any objective or commonly subscribed to means of measuring this excellence, leaving particularly finicky partners the freedom to impose their own sometimes over-exacting standards covering not only the content of routine correspondence but also its line-by-line style – a factor which imposes on fee earners the sometimes demoralizing responsibility of second guessing what is in the mind of their matter partner. Time is another factor. It is often simpler for the matter partner to undertake themselves the work they wish to delegate rather than risk having to correct mistakes and coach the assistant if something goes wrong.

» Among those partners who go to the other extreme and delegate the operational responsibility for the matter almost wholly to a senior associate, productivity and greater efficiency can be undermined because a proper framework of expectations and guidelines is not provided. In the opinion of a number of people we interviewed, fee earners almost have to assess the standards and expectations they work to by "osmosis."

» All of these factors combine in creating a number of difficulties in managing the careers and the effective performance of fee earners – although it should be stressed that these are not unique to this firm or the legal profession. While there is an almost universal consensus that this firm is exceptional in the high standards it sets in recruiting and supporting legal trainees, this organizational support does not seem to extend beyond the point where they qualify. Fee earners are, in effect, left in a "sink or swim" situation. Partners are either unwilling or unable to devote billable time to "bring on" fee earners who do not meet their standards, leaving the laggards to be gradually weeded out through lack of promotion or dismissal. There appears to be a body of opinion (probably very small) that applauds this form of social Darwinism. However, concerns do exist among partners across all sectors that a discrete body of fee earners are lost to the firm who have technical expertise that the firm needs at partner level but who lack the personality and self-management to compete in a culture where the "halo effect" often dictates promotion prospects.

» The sink or swim culture may also be losing the firm people who also meet the current criteria for partner. There appears to be very little incentive to move from junior to senior assistant status other than it is the next rung on the ladder to making partner. Indeed, talented assistants who have the ability to manage work effectively without direct supervision wind up overloaded with work that otherwise would have been allocated to their less well developed colleagues – work for which, in many cases, they will receive little or no formal recognition, in terms of client or partner feedback, since virtually all the people we interviewed acknowledged that partners generally at the firm lack the ability to praise or otherwise recognize work they approve of.

» Even the fee earners who are happy to accept the rather artificial promotion from junior to senior associate as a sign that they are on the road to the top, feel there is a recognition that the position in itself provides little motivation or satisfaction to a talented junior who, for whatever reason, does not wish to become a partner.

» Thus the shortcomings in the role are justifiable if fee earners see the prospect of making partner directly ahead of them, but if at any point the prospect becomes dimmer (for whatever reason) they are very likely to leave. The central office usually accommodates this form of wastage but in smaller offices, where prospects are more tightly constrained and local competition is more intense, a number of talented fee earners have been lost that the local practice found hard to replace.

» There appears (again based purely on the feedback we received) to be very little recognition among partners at the firm that good performance is linked to any motivation other than money – and that fee earners might work better for one partner rather than another because that partner has a better management style. Although everyone stresses that the firm lives up to its reputation as a friendly place to work, this does not always appear to extend to partners recognizing that even very talented fee earners by the firms' current standards occasionally experience dips in their performance for various reasons.

» Two final conclusions are worth stressing. While there appears to be a general consensus that raising the level of non-billable time is desirable, partners may prefer to use this time to engage in speculative marketing, which will bring them and the firm direct financial rewards, rather than coaching and developing fee earners, where the link with improved commercial results is not reflected in either their personal status or earnings. There is also a consensus that the proportion of non-contentious work is likely to increase in the next 5–10 years and that this growth will come from sectors where new skills like project management and teambuilding will be required as well as a more balanced division of roles between matter partners and fee earners.

Issues

» Do the shortcomings in the current practice of supervision and delegation stem from a lack of skills, outdated attitudes or organizational and marketplace constraints? The feedback we received suggests that the problem is linked to all three causes. Most (but not all) of the people we interviewed felt that partners would benefit from a "template" of good practice combined with a few basic principles of coaching; however, an almost similar proportion stressed that partners would not implement this good practice on a day to day basis if their willingness to do so was not recognized by the firm and if market pressures and client expectations left them little scope to do so.

» Should this session, and indeed others in the series, be confined to individual skills training or should it also incorporate a facil-itated discussion about the firm's organizational development? Most of the people we interviewed agreed that any measure which reduced the inconsistencies in partners' management styles would be welcome; however, they are all too aware that the context in which they exercise their skills is likely to change in the next 10 years and that any framework of good practice outlined during the session will need to anticipate these changes.

Example 2: Local community primary school

As part of a government-funded initiative to promote better work–life balance policies in organizations, a local community primary school sought to increase its attainment targets by promoting work practices that would better motivate a professional workforce marked by high absenteeism and regular sickness absence.

The initiative was personally led and championed by the head teacher. Although he started the process with an open mind about its remit, he had in mind some kind of flexible working hours package that would act both as a recruitment and retention aid.

An extensive organizational needs analysis was undertaken to assess whether this type of outcome was, in fact, what was needed. The senior staff (head and deputy head), three governors, two office administrators and a cross-section of teachers undertook a simple structured interview (see box below) to assess their own definition of work–life balance and what personal and school-initiated measures would help them achieve it. These findings were discussed and elaborated during an activity learning day involving all but three of the total staff.

The feedback from this exercise revealed a more complex problem. The office administrators, both married with children, had "family friendly" work–life balance needs that could be met using conventional flexible working packages (see ExpressExec titles *Flexible and Virtual Working* and *Recruiting and Retaining People*).

The single teaching staff, who constituted the majority, were a different matter. Work–life balance for them meant being able to "switch off" work mentally when they chose to. New to the profession, vocationally driven and without the diversions of family life, they took home concerns and worries about classroom issues and problems. Their inability to switch off was not helped by the fact that the school had been under intense scrutiny for not achieving its attainment targets, leading to pressure across the board, and that they felt unable to seek help and share problems with more experienced colleagues.

Flexible working patterns were therefore only a partial solution. For example, making more space and time for extra-curricular tasks to be undertaken on the school's premises was not necessarily welcomed by teachers because planning classroom activities and marking assignments was something they preferred to do in peace and quiet at home. What they required was the freedom to switch *on* work when and where they wanted and to switch *off* work in the same way.

This perspective changed the whole thrust of the initiative (see second box below). More emphasis was placed on fostering better team working and internal benchmarking. The time spent on joint planning and consultation exercises was reviewed as well as how and when staff interacted in the common room.

STRUCTURED INTERVIEW (PRIMARY SCHOOL)

1 How do you "see" work–life balance?
2 What do you consider to be the most desired outcome/benefit of a work–life initiative at your school:

» For you?
» For the school?

3 What needs to happen to achieve this outcome:

» For you?
» For the school?

ORGANIZATIONAL NEEDS ANALYSIS (PRIMARY SCHOOL)

The challenge as we see it

The extensive organizational needs analysis we undertook at the school during Stage One, supported by the activity learning day, has given us an insight into how teaching staff see work–life balance personally – and what work-based and personal factors inhibit or support it. The key issues are:

» Staff need to "de-role" as teachers before they feel able to unwind and relax. They feel unable to do so within close proximity to the school premises. The journey home, on the bus or in the train, is a key part of this process.

» Staff feel unable to mentally "switch off" from work because the opportunity to share and resolve issues that they feel reflect on their own professional performance and integrity as teachers is often lacking in a busy school schedule. In part, this is due to the unavoidable (from the school's point of view) pressures imposed in achieving attainment targets and meeting the external demands of a highly regulated public sector. In part, it is because the internal processes designed to promote a collective exchange of views and solutions are not currently yielding the desired benefits.

» The issue is not so much related to what work activities take place on and off school premises and in school time as to staff feeling they have the ability to switch on and off work at times of their own choosing. Many individuals, for example, prefer to plan their classroom activities at home. But they want to choose the time and circumstances themselves, rather than feeling so overwhelmed that the issues are forcibly on their minds at times when they want to enjoy non-work activities.

The focus for our intervention in Stage Two

We would like to take what we now know about how staff define work-life balance and examine the internal processes designed to foster organizational learning and teamwork in this light. These might include:

» staff induction and training;
» staff meetings;
» staff social events;
» the use of "Inset" days;
» professional mentoring;
» use of the staff common room; and

> » general opportunities for serendipity in the course of day-to-day work.
>
> By identifying ways in which these processes can be better informed by, and act on, the personal and professional pressures felt by staff, we hope to restore a level of control over their working lives that will enable them to enjoy their leisure time and return to work each day refreshed and better able to reach their own and the school's attainment targets.

DESIGN: CAUSE AND EFFECT

Feedback from TNA and ONA exercises will enable you to pinpoint the parameters, aims and desired outcomes of the initiatives. Within this broad framework, you will also have at your disposal a variety of specific training tools, techniques and exercises that can help tailor the material or external contribution more closely to the needs of participants. These include any or all of the following.

Pre-program preparation

Management development programs nearly always take place when time for participants is at a premium. Rare is the instance when the HR practitioner has the group together in one place for long enough to achieve everything he or she wants to. It is therefore important that when the group assemble, they "hit the deck running."

In management training terms, this means any or all of the following.

» Participants have a basic understanding of the issues, concepts or techniques under scrutiny.
» They have a basic understanding or consensus of what the program is designed to achieve and what the most likely collective or individual outputs will be.
» They have a clear idea of what their own learning needs and objectives are.
» They have illustrative examples drawn from their own or their work unit's experiences that can be used as "live" case studies at given points during the program.

Some of this may have been achieved using the broader framework of individual appraisal adopted by the organization. This is discussed in more detail in the ExpressExec title *Developing the Individual*. However thorough appraisal systems are in the organization, however, the needs of both the individual and the group need to be framed in the context of the program they will be attending.

This might involve a pre-course reading assignment or a short questionnaire or a request to reflect on their own experiences – or a combination of all three. Whatever the choice, the exercise should be simple, not lasting more than 15 minutes, so that it is not perceived to be eating into the individual's working time.

EXAMPLE

In Example 1 above, an international firm of lawyers set up a partner training initiative. The first session covered basic delegation techniques, so that junior and senior associates' performance could be enhanced by better briefing and appraisal from their managing partner.

The training needs analysis exercise had indicated that the specific delegation skills of partners was only part of the problem. Equally important was the overall position of associates or "fee earners" in the firm, in particular a "sink or swim" culture in which promising associates were loaded with more and more work while those trailing behind were left on the wayside.

As a preparation for a two-day workshop on delegation, partners were circulated with an article based on a radical approach to "associate democracy" adopted by a real firm in the United States, Anderson Kill, Olick & Oshinsky. Under this approach, associates were not only given voting rights to help determine pay scales (including those of partners) but to contribute to decisions about associate promotions.

Participants were given the following instructions:

Take 10 minutes to read the article. After reflecting on the radical approach to "democracy" adopted by Anderson Kill, spend no more than 20 minutes to consider:

(a) What aspects of the policy might be applicable at your own firm (for example, the greater involvement of fee earners in key decisions or greater transparency in earnings, both of which resulted in higher retention rates at Anderson Kill)?

(b) What aspects of the policy are not, in your opinion, applicable at your own firm?

(c) What implications to your own approach to supervision and delegation might there be if your response to (a) was implemented at your own firm?

Please fax or e-mail your considerations to the training department no later than five days before the program.

Bring a copy of these with you for discussion. Expect to be asked to justify them.

The purpose of the exercise was two-fold. First, to engage participants as early in the process as possible. The TNA exercise had already indicated that most partners were very conservative about the role of associates. Reacting to the radical approach taken by a respected US firm in the opening session obliged them to justify their stance rather than take it for granted.

Secondly, to place the highly focused aim of improving delegation skills into a broader organizational context. Largely as a result of the discussion surrounding the pre-program exercise, participants agreed that in addition to individual delegation skills, most partners also required team building and project leadership training, both to reflect the changing nature of the firm's work and as a means of ''bringing on'' associates and thus improving their ability to meet client needs more directly (see TNA report above).

Formal presentation

The heart of any program is usually a formal presentation by an expert in the field outlining a new technique, tool, concept or approach to management. Choosing the appropriate contributor is dealt with a little later in this chapter, but in an age where organizational learning and internally generated innovation are a priority, the presentation is usually the start rather than the end of the process.

As discussed in some detail in Chapter 2, formal presentations act like a stone in a pond. It is participants' reaction to the input that created the learning dynamic, not the input itself. It is very rare that knowledge or skill-based experts possess either the ability or the inclination to tailor what they say to the specific needs of the group. That task nearly always falls on the HR practitioner or external consultant that sources and briefs the expert.

EXAMPLE

The newly appointed chief executive of an insurance company championed the idea of a "forum," meeting once a quarter, which would provide a venue where the boardroom directors and senior functional directors could learn from external good practice and share ideas and concerns.

The group was designed to be self-sustaining in raising issues for discussion. Topics were not fixed in advance. Rather the choice of future issues emerged out of the participants' reactions and responses to the presentation of the previous expert.

For example, the group expressed interest in how mature companies re-motivated themselves to compete effectively with newer players in the industry. The organizers brought in one of the leading academic experts on this topic, Professor John Stopford from London Business School.

During Stopford's session, the opinion was expressed that re-motivating a jaded workforce was easily achievable during a period when the industry or sector in which the organization was active was in growth; but far harder, as in the case of the insurance industry at the time, when it was in crisis.

To discuss this issue, the organizers brought in the boardroom director at a leading European airline who had recently overseen a reduction of annual costs amounting to £200mn a year. His outline of how the company had sustained staff performance during the cuts generated a consensus that while sustaining basic perfor-mance was possible in these circumstances, sustaining innovation was almost impossible.

A careful balance was always maintained between focusing on strategic outcomes that benefited the company in the short term and therefore increased the credibility of the forum in the eyes of participants and senior managers, and the project's primary task of providing members with a broader perspective of their role and a source of personal development.

The role of event "sponsor," for example, was used both to develop individuals in the group and to ensure outside experts set the good practice outlined in the session in the context of the group's specific needs. By giving a different member of the forum in each session responsibility for liaising with the organizers, briefing the speaker and hosting the event, the organizers ensured that there was a high level of individual and collective ownership of the issues being discussed.

Simulations and scenarios

As a support to an external presentation, or a stand alone exercise in its own right, exercises based on simulations or scenarios allow participants, either individually or in teams, to test their acquired knowledge or capability in an exercise which simulates as closely as possible a likely crisis or contentious situation.

The learning in these exercises only sinks home if each individual believes that the situation he or she is placed in is plausible and could really happen to the organization or work unit. Countering the "it couldn't happen here" factor is essential if the project is not to prove a wasted effort.

For this reason, the authors argue strongly that off-the-shelf simula-tions rarely work effectively. Time and effort should be spent on the initial research and design to ensure the following:

» the exercise should test that the participants have acquired the specific capabilities or expert knowledge that is the focus of the overall program (see example below);

» it should be set in the context of an upcoming or recent event that is likely to occur or has occurred to the work unit or organization (e.g. a merger, product development launch, government initiative, alliance or relocation) – the plausibility of the scenario should be validated by at least one member of the organization's strategic management team;

» the characters in the simulation (senior managers, chief executive, trade union leaders, external experts) should be real and their actions based on known character traits or management styles – if possible the individuals on whom the characters are based should be present either during the simulation or when its output is assessed; and

» the exercise should carried out in "real time" – in other words the participants should be subject to the same time and resource pressures as they would be if the situation being simulated was real.

Example

As part of the "Serving the Community" initiative (see above), the Hong Kong government wanted to test the ability of the deputy directors of its key utility services (fire, police, urban services, hospital services etc.) to communicate effectively with the public and other key stakeholders during a crisis.

The senior policy managers had no doubt that their key services could work across boundaries to deal with the effects of a natural disaster. Hong Kong is one of the few major urban centers built on the side of a mountain in a climate marked at certain times of the year by high winds and torrential rain. Landslides are a constant danger and the government possessed, and still possesses, the geo-technical expertise to pinpoint danger areas and respond swiftly to events.

What the government wanted to test was the ability of a project team made up from representatives of different departments to manage the flow of information to a better informed and better read community. The introduction of a directly elected legislative assembly (LegCo), coupled with a boom in new Chinese-language newspapers and broadcasting stations, meant that government services were subject to a scrutiny that their civil servants had never experienced and were not equipped to respond to. This had been demonstrated vividly in 1994 when a major landslide at Hong Kong's second port Aberdeen, involving scores of deaths and injuries, had attracted unprecedented criticism of the government by the media when senior civil servants had tried to lay the blame at the door of individual landowners.

The following year, the Hong Kong Civil Service Training Department was commissioned to run a training exercise simulating a landslide for the deputies who would take over key departments in the run up to the transfer of sovereignty to China in 1997. The department had run exercises of this kind before, but this time the focus of the simulation would be crisis *communications*, not crisis management.

The department, in conjunction with consultants from the Poon Kam Kai Institute of Management (PKKI) at the University of Hong Kong, researched the simulation thoroughly. The senior manager of the geo-technical department was consulted to pinpoint the location for a likely landslide that would cause the maximum disruption to daily city life. The chosen spot straddled the main highway into town for commuter traffic from the New Territories as well as access roads servicing the principal docks as well as a school and hospital. A tunnel servicing a much used branch line of Hong Kong's mass transit railway also passed directly under the slope.

PKKI consultants interviewed the LegCo member responsible for the district to check how she would react. Correspondents from a selection of the territory's principal English- and Chinese-language newspapers and radio stations took part in the exercise. The exercise simulated the first six hours of what would occur if a landslide occurred at this spot in the early hours of a busy weekday morning, blocking access not only to rush hour traffic entering the city and the port area but also to the local school and hospital.

Participants not only had to work together to form a crisis team to manage the chaos, but explain what they were doing to the press. The exercise was designed to highlight inconsistencies in public statements and a failure by the team to address key stakeholders, such as LegCo members and representatives from the school or hospital. A landslide in the early hours was followed in the scenario by the collapse of the railway tunnel running under the slope, killing two people and bringing all mass transit traffic to a halt.

The geo-technical department chose this scenario because the collapse of a tunnel in these circumstances was unlikely, and therefore difficult to predict, but theoretically possible. The scenario was designed to force the team to tread the very fine line between claiming that it would have been hard for them to predict and therefore anticipate the collapse of the tunnel (true in fact) and being seen to use this claim to abrogate all responsibility for the consequences.

Participants were drip fed events as they occurred and had to make key decisions on the basis of imperfect information. Consultants playing key stakeholders as well as real-life news correspondents bombarded the room that acted as the crisis center with calls and messages, forcing participants to either make statements without the full facts being available or to stonewall inquiries. After the exercise finished, extensive plenary and syndicate discussions (see below) distilled the good (and bad) practice emerging from the exercise and measuring participants' actions against those of counterparts in comparable crises.

Outdoor/action learning

As an alternative to classroom simulations and scenarios, an increasingly popular means of testing key team building or project leadership skills is through an outdoor or outplaced exercise.

David Charlton, a former senior manager at ICI and Mars, pioneered outdoor training in the UK by founding Celmi Experience, a residential outdoor training center in the mountainous natural park of Snowdonia in Wales. He argues that the learning potential of outdoor activity lies in the way the "natural inputs" like topography, climate, time of day and seasonal changes transform conventional "human inputs" like attitudes to designs and rules, perceived constraints and the way we review and measure progress (see Table 6.1).

"Whatever way the outdoors is managed for experiential learning and leadership development the human response to the elements and the explosion of senses add a huge set of variables to their existing larder of experiences. In addition the intellectual, emotional and physical response of an individual will change and change again in relation to other individuals' changing responses, or as groups interact with groups. The permutations of the learning experience are as endless as they are powerful in outdoor programs."

Table 6.1 Inputs to outdoor experiential learning. Source: Charlton, D. (1990) "Developing leaders using the outdoors." *Frontiers of Leadership*, Blackwell, Oxford.

Natural inputs		Orchestration
THE OUTDOORS		THE PROVIDER
Topography		Designs and rules
Climate/weather		Constraints, objectives
Remoteness		Interventions
Time of day/night		Imagination
Seasonal changes		Creativity
Flora/fauna		Reviewing and facilitating learning
	PARTICIPANTS	
	Human response	
	Group responses	
	Individual responses	
	Mental	
	Physical	
	Emotional	

Charlton's advocacy for the possibilities of outdoor management are reflected closely in the reasons why Michael Useem, director of the Center for Leadership and Change Management at the University of Pennsylvania's Wharton School of Management, chose to take 20 trekkers, including MBA graduates and mid-career executives, on a mountain climb in the Himalayas in 2001 to heighten their understanding of "what true leadership is all about."

In a write-up of the expedition, published in *Harvard Business Review*, he commented:

"We made the trip to Mount Everest not because it could teach us things about leadership that we couldn't have learned elsewhere but because the lessons learned there would have far greater urgency. When problems arose, they could rapidly worsen – or be resolved – depending on how quickly people put into action those theoretical leadership concepts."

However, David Charlton has an important proviso, one that distinguishes whether true lessons will be learned or the exercise just proves wasted money and effort.

"A crucial part of the planning of an outdoor program is the setting of clear learning objectives. These need to be established and understood by the organizer so the outdoor experience can be targeted with optimum orchestration to obtain the best results. There is little point in sending a group or an individual on an outdoor learning experience if they return with insights and skills that they are unable or unwilling to use in the workplace."

It is also worth stressing that it is not always necessary to send groups of managers into the wilds to create the psychological interaction set out by Charlton in Table 6.1. Conventional rules and constraints can be challenged using any activity that intellectually or physically engages the individual or group. Similarly, any location that is unrelated to everyday routine provides a potential venue for a transference of learning.

EXAMPLE

In Example 2 above, a local community primary school pinpointed in an organizational needs analysis that young single teachers working for the school were unable to mentally "switch off" from their work at the end of the day because they felt unable to share issues and problems in the classrooms with their colleagues or senior teachers. Part of the problem was that there was little opportunity for the workforce as a whole to engage in joint social or development activity.

Accordingly one of the school's "Inset" (training) days was set aside for a team building exercise. Constraints on time and the school curriculum meant that only one day was available for the workshop. Budget constraints also made it impossible for the group to stay overnight in a training center or hotel. In addition while the school's young single teachers, many of them from Australia and New Zealand, were happy about an out of doors activity, the administrative staff were more daunted. There was a danger that they would be "de-skilled" by an activity requiring fitness and agility that they felt they lacked. The non-residential constraints also made travel to an out of town location hard to achieve.

A TNA exercise conducted by the work–life balance consultants organizing the event indicated that the majority of professional staff enjoyed out of hours socializing in pubs and bars. So the organizers hit on the idea of hiring a private room in a local bar and designing the team building day around a series of traditional British pub games: darts, skittles, shove-halfpenny, quoits and table football.

Mixed groups of teachers and administrators were organized in teams and competed with each other in each of the games. During the activity, each team was asked to observe what role every member played. After the event, they were organized into syndicate groups to discuss the extent to which the roles adopted by each team member in the game (expert, supporter, coordinator etc.) corresponded to the role he or she played at work. In a final plenary session, the group examined how they could transfer the culture of support and encouragement they had demonstrated in the games to the workplace.

Given that a major issue raised by the TNA exercise had been the inability of young teaching staff to mentally "switch off" their work after hours, and that this had been aggravated by an unwillingness to share classroom problems with their colleagues, the activity day went a long way towards raising mutual support and mentoring as a key professional issue.

Syndicate and plenary discussion

Syndicate and plenary discussion, designed to enable participants to respond to the contribution or activity at the start of the program, lies at the heart of what used to be called the learning organization. Yet it is often treated as a cosmetic afterthought, little more than another form of Q&A.

In the authors' experience, even the best-intended syndicate or plenary sessions are wasted or undermined for any or all of the following reasons.

» The task assigned to the group in the wake of the formal activity or presentation seizes participants at their most engaged and intellectually motivated (provided the presenter or organizer has done his or her job properly). Yet assignments at this crucial point are commonly unfocused or banal.

» Because participants are at their most engaged and motivated, syndicate and plenary discussions provide the best opportunity for capturing original thought in its purest and rawest form. It is the insights and concepts that arise from participants' immediate response to the issue or approach under question that are the richest source of innovation and original thinking wholly unique to the sponsoring organization. Yet the flipcharts, notes and impromptu slides that net this thinking are often stuffed, unseen and unshared, in the back seat of the HR practitioner's car; or, worse, immediately trashed or left for the conference center to dispose of.

» For the same reason, the discussions assume a far greater significance if participants feel their intellectual output will be assessed or responded to by the organization's senior managers. In some circumstances, it is possible to arrange for the chief executive or strategic director to sit in on the final plenary session and formally respond to the output of each syndicate. At the very least, the material should form the basis of a formal document or intranet file that is presented to the senior manager, who commits to provide a response.

EXAMPLE

In March 1997, the University of Oulu in Finland organized an overseas residential module in China for participants on its executive MBA program. The first week of a fortnight visit was spent in south China, in the provincial capital of Guangzhou. Participants attended lectures on Chinese culture and society given by professors at the local university, but most of their time was taken up visiting locally based businesses. These were a mixture of state-run enterprises such as the Guangzhou Petrochemical Company, and subsidiaries of Finnish companies established in South China such as Outokumpu Copper Tube.

To ensure that insight and lessons were captured systematically, a syndicate approach was adopted by the organizers. Participants were divided into research syndicates, each of which investigated an aspect of the operations of the organizations to be visited (such as marketing, technology, human resources and distribution) and compared the different practices of local Chinese enterprises and firms from their own country.

The second week was spent at the Robert Black College of the University of Hong Kong. Participants attended a series of sessions taught by tutors from the Poon Kam Kai Institute of Management, during which they tested the results of their trip against the perspectives of a series of guest speakers including senior managers from well-established Finnish firms in the region such as Kone Elevators and Tam Glass.

The material gathered at the end of the visit was considerable. So that it was assimilated in a practical context, the original syndicates were set the task of making a presentation to the director of the Finnish Business Council on the guidelines that should be published by all Finnish firms wishing to set up in the region. The recommendations made by the syndicates formed the basis of all guidelines subsequently developed by the Council.

CHOOSING AND BRIEFING A SUPPLIER

In Chapter 2, we argued that there was no single model for how and when internal HR experts used suppliers. In some organizations, the training needs analysis and design of the initiative are undertaken by an in-house specialist, and those parts of the program to be delivered by external suppliers are tendered out to an exact specification. In others, internal HR practitioners act solely as a broker and internal contact point.

Table 6.2 provides a summary of the trade-offs. It suggests that the perspective of the internal HR practitioner in providing an accurate

Table 6.2   Inside or out: The pros and cons. Source: J. Lammiman,1998.

Function	Internal	External
Definition of need/training needs analysis	Ability to reflect real need	Ability to see the wood for the trees
Design of program	Access to key internal stakeholders, data and strategy	Strong remit to act where internal HR staff might be disenfranchised
Facilitation of program	Closer to the real need/access to internal expertise	Broader knowledge of what does and does not work
Delivery of program	Less expensive if run in-house; more control over the tailoring of external contributions to internal needs. Internal speakers link any external contribution to business imperatives and, used effectively, provide greater ownership and prompt deeper discussion of internal issues	Provides a neutral environment which allows participants to step out of their roles. External speakers provide insight into how the issue or topic is perceived or practiced by other companies and allow participants to see the issue from a different mental framework

perspective of both the training and organizational needs governing the initiative is invaluable. The unalloyed view of front line managers may be too close to the need. The untempered perspective of external consultants or academics may be too distant. The experience of the authors is that the parameter of any management development initiative is best informed by a balanced combination of all three (see Table 6.2).

Equally demanding is the choice of the supplier. Specialist consultancy services are now provided by an extraordinarily diverse mix of suppliers, including university business schools, independent management centers, specialist training consultancies, generalist management consultancies and a host of sole practitioners and partnerships.

In the past decade, the distinguishing features of each have narrowed. Large consultancies like Bain & Co and the Boston Consulting Group have matched the top business schools in pioneering new research and ideas, most notably business process re-engineering. The schools themselves have recruited a new breed of client directors, who act as gatekeepers and pulsetakers in helping customers assess their needs and sourcing the right faculty.

In 1992 George Rabstejneck, president of the well-known US consultancy Harbridge House, commented: "We are far better equipped to handle the process of analyzing companies' needs. But we cannot compete with the brand image of schools like Harvard and Stanford and that image is nearly always linked to the reputation of the faculty."

Five years later, the president of the international school IMD in Lausanne, Peter Lorange, responded in this way:

"Schools will need to follow a consulting firm's way of operating. But while consulting firms have also performed high-quality research on critical issues, and while their raison d'être is often to help bridge the gap between strategic priorities and specific behaviors, the distinctive competence of business schools should be in engineering executive learning. There must also be an underlying network of relationships, primarily between each firm and a business school but also among partners in consortia, leading to genuine learning solutions."

This is all very well if you have the resources and internal expertise to set up a sophisticated consortium of the kind described in the next chapter. However, most HR practitioners wind up having to choose between suppliers who may share the same expert knowledge or tools but who have widely differing client liaison skills.

The box below provides a few common criteria. The decision will often turn on their understanding of your own sector or industry and their ability to tailor off-the-shelf tools or techniques to the specific needs of the program. Our own experience is that it is often possible to find suppliers with one or the other but harder to find those with both.

WHAT TO LOOK FOR IN CHOOSING A SUPPLIER

» Do they have a history of work (and a track record of success) in the area or industry?

» Do they have skill in client liaison and the ability to identify or question your true development needs?

» Will you get access to the real McCoy – senior faculty or consultants with expert research and teaching ability – and not just an understudy?

» Do they just "press button B" – outlining general statements of truth and established points of principle – or are they prepared to get to know the individual or organization well enough to use their intellectual resources to uncover hidden insights?

» Is the "big noise" – the star member of faculty or practice – prepared to work with you to tailor or design the optimum program or will you wind up with a verbal synopsis of their latest book or research program?

» Whose diary is it anyway? – are you calling the tune on timings and venue or are they merely fitting you in?

Source: J. Lammiman, 1998.

KEY LEARNING POINTS

» Linking management development initiatives to strategic goals can be achieved in a number of ways. The most common are based on scenario-based projections of the future, an assessment of critical success factors, an assessment of the human resource capabilities of the organization, and an assessment of the likely future skills and capabilities that will be needed by key professional staff.

» Definitions of management skills used across organizations and sectors should be tested and re-evaluated against the meaning understood by managers and staff in the work units from which participants will be drawn.

» The goals of the initiative should be tested and re-evaluated against the specific needs of participants using a formal training needs analysis exercise. Formal presentations, scenarios, case studies and assignations should only be drawn up or designed *after* these findings have been taken into account.

» A brief pre-program exercise or assignment will provide participants "on the day" with a common psychological start point. It will also encourage participants to arrive with examples, insights and (if requested) personal case studies that can be drawn on to illustrate the concepts or good practice under scrutiny.

» Scenarios or assignments should be designed specifically for the initiative and not "off the shelf" to enable participants to see how the concepts or good practice apply in their own or their organization's circumstances, thus ensuring that the learning is genuinely transferable.

» Effectively designed syndicate or plenary discussion following any formal presentation or assignment is the most important means of achieving "double loop" learning. It will not only help participants iron out disagreements about the conclusions to be drawn and help them transfer the learning; by prompting them to reinterpret and re-evaluate the concepts or good practice in the light of their own or their employer's circumstances, it will help to generate firm-specific concepts and insights that will prove an invaluable resource to the organization as a whole.

» For this reason, every use should be made of new Internet technology to capture, codify and disseminate the output or conclusions of the initiative, not only to participants but to a wider management audience. As we saw in Chapter 4, the full potential of intranets, discussional databases and interactive e-mail exchanges to promote collaborative learning has yet to be fully realized by any organization.

In Practice

- » Corporate "universities" in practice
- » Tailored degrees in practice
- » Consortium programs in practice

An abiding problem confronting large corporations is how to position broad-based management education in the context of the organization's specific needs. Swing the balance too much down the tailored route and managers will lack the lateral knowledge they need to learn from new concepts and good practice outside the boundaries of their own organization or industry. Swing too far the other way and they will be unable to apply the concepts or techniques they have acquired back in the workplace.

This chapter looks at how a number of models designed to bridge the gap - internally run corporate learning centers, consortium programs undertaken with a number of partners outside the parent industry, and tailored degrees developed with top business schools - have worked in practice.

CORPORATE "UNIVERSITIES" IN PRACTICE

The most perfect form of the first model is fulfilled by the "corporate universities" of the United States, of which there are now well over 100. When these first emerged in the early 1980s, pioneered by large corporations like General Electric and Motorola, they were seen as a direct challenge to the university schools which, unlike their counterparts in Europe, had a virtual monopoly on management education and could afford to maintain academic constraints on degree education in the face of little or no competition from independent schools like Henley or Ashridge in the UK and INSEAD or IMD on the mainland.

This seems to be borne out by the fact that the development of company or industry-specific MBAs of the type pioneered by European schools has been taken up by a number of corporate universities in the States while being resisted fiercely by the conventional universities. However, a survey of over 90 deans of corporate universities in the States, together with 10 from other parts of the world, by the AACSB, the accrediting body for US business schools, suggests that the rise of corporate universities represents an opportunity rather than a risk to their traditional counterparts.

Although some corporate universities are attempting to develop degree awarding powers themselves, the survey suggests a decisive shift in corporate universities' thinking towards developing joint degree programs with other institutions of higher education. Forty percent of corporate universities plan to grant degrees in partnership with accredited higher education institutions, mostly in business administration, computer science, engineering and finance. A further 32% have linked with executive education units, with another 15% planning to form such a link in the next two years.

The Concord School of Management (formerly the Arthur D. Little Institute) is a typical example. Founded and run by the international management consultancy, it grew up wholly outside the academic traditions of American business education and was started almost by accident in the 1960s. The consultancy was working with a state-owned Nigerian company that needed to train a large number of its indigenous managers but could not find a suitable institution in Africa. So Arthur D. Little set up its own at its headquarters in Boston and quickly found that its down to earth attitude to management education appealed to managers who did not necessarily work for client companies.

Traditionally, the ADL Institute used a combination of its own consultants and top professors brought in from a variety of neighboring universities in Boston. In 1998, it formed an alliance with Boston College and the programs it offers are designed, taught and accredited in collaboration with the College.

The Concord School of Management is exceptional in the extent to which it has opened up its expertise to outside students. Its Masters program is cited side by side with those of its more conventional Boston neighbors and with the exception that its own consultants teach on its programs, there is now little to distinguish it from any other US business school.

Corporately yours

General Electric's "university" at Crotonville is a different matter entirely. It exists entirely to educate and develop its global workforce of 222,000 in 11 different companies, in sessions popularly known in the company as "workouts." The Crotonville training facility is one hour's drive from New York City, situated on the Hudson River. Five thousand GE employees are trained there every year. The facility has over 200 beds and the majority of the faculty are senior GE managers – including ex-CEO Jack Welch, who teaches leadership – supported by a small number of external academics and consultants. "We source faculty from outside, but good as they are, only a handful are useful to GE,'' says Steve Kerr, Vice-President, Corporate Management Development. ''We can help the good ones adapt to GE, but not the bulk of them.''

Thirty permanent staff are employed at Crotonville (compared with about 100 at the facilities run by Motorola and AT&T) with another six in Asia and six in Europe coordinating programs in external sites. Their mission is to ''identify, create and transfer organizational learning to enhance GE's growth and competitiveness worldwide. Specifically, this is broken down into four goals:

» provide growth and development to GE professionals through education and training;
» transfer best practices, corporate initiatives, and change management concepts and serve as the primary integrating mechanism of training across the businesses;
» partner with the business to educate, develop and build with their customers and external constituencies; and
» be a major conduit for transmitting GE's culture and values.

Although Crotonville does teach staff from non-GE companies, these tend to be customers and suppliers. The focus of the programs, usually lasting between one week and four, is focused entirely on doing business the GE way. Since 1992 the emphasis has been on managing accelerating change, internal corporate TQM initiatives, business team training, leverage with customers and suppliers and achieving a global reach for the business.

GE's facility at Crotonville is at the far end of the polarity between those that train in-house and those who contract out, but internal training facilities on both sides of the Atlantic share many of its characteristics.

The Ericsson Management Institute in Stockholm targets the telecoms corporation's top 2,500 managers, providing a focus for networking and leadership development enriched by participants from different functions and cultures. Like Crotonville, it ensures a worldwide consistency in quality and management style that Ericsson feels it needs to be a global player as well as reinforcing Ericsson's corporate values and vision. ''We started in 1989 when we felt we didn't need the sort of diversity offered by the bigger business schools,'' says Knut

Johansen, head of the Institute. "With over half of our 90,000 people based outside Sweden, there was already enough on our programs.

"We have tried working in consortiums with other companies, normally our strategic alliance partners. These get great support, but we've been unable to really get them going. Finding the right people in the company and the business school to run consortiums is critical – and rare."

In Britain, the NatWest Education and Learning Centre at Heythrop Park in Oxfordshire, with 270 bedrooms, has a similar goal – as the Head of Group Human Resources explains:

"The objectives of the Centre are numerous. Uppermost are to provide a platform for Group leaders to achieve change and promote Group vision and values. Research and consultancy on organizational development, education, development and training issues are carried out there, and business education in partnership with UK business schools is delivered there. Problem-solving through facilitated work-groups involving, for example, the top 500 executives is coordinated, as well as 'blue-sky thinking' on new products and strategic alliances. Some of these are carried out with our partners. A recent five-day retreat, for example, involved our people with their counterparts at A.T. Kearney and British Telecom, exploring what leadership will mean in 10 years time with the people who are going to inherit it."

WHAT DO THE BEST CORPORATE LEARNING CENTERS LOOK LIKE?

» Underpin globalization of corporate values and corporate culture.
» Achieve reach and continuing support through use of leading edge education and communications technology.
» Depend on and involve line management and external faculty.
» Have very few or no internal "fixed" faculty.
» Act as a center of "knowledge networks" (internal and external to the company).

» "Bricks and mortar" is not the main issue – accessibility is the
important thing.
» Owned by the line, rather than one key figure (e.g. the CEO) or
Human Resources.
» Assert separate identity from traditional HRD/Training depart-
ments and define scope/territory clearly to avoid competition
with HRD/Training.
» Have some key measurables and are accountable to the business.

Source: European Foundation for Management Development

Heythrop Park is closer to the model for corporate learning centers
defined by the European Foundation for Management Development
(efmd) in the box above than Crotonville. Very few corporations
have the resources – and perhaps the arrogance – of General Electric,
Motorola and AT&T to train their managers entirely in-house. They may
have the numbers and the diversity of functions and ethnic origins
among their managerial workforce to attempt a general management
education within their own borders but most companies regard it as
necessary and perhaps wiser to enter into some kind of partnership
with an external supplier.

The Cable & Wireless MBA for Telecommunications, for example (see
Chapter 8), was designed by faculty from Henley Management College
and C&W's own faculty working for the company's own internal college
based just outside Coventry. The general management modules are
taught by Henley tutors and those relating to the telecommunications
industry by Cable & Wireless College staff. Similarly, residential modules
relating to general management topics take place on the Henley campus
while those relating specifically to telecommunications take place at
the C&W College.

What, summing up, is the difference between a corporate "university" and a corporate training department? A good definition was
recently supplied in a report published in 2002 by the European
Foundation for Management Development (see box above).

A corporate university, the report stresses, differs from the company
training department because it is part of the organization's strategy to
change itself. It reports to the Board, not the HR department. It not

only trains employees in new skills, it is also the organization's agency for deciding what training will be needed, what knowledge will be required and how innovation can best be encouraged and focused.

It will pioneer new training and learning technologies and methods. It will cultivate strategic relationships with a few lead suppliers and wider network of occasional ones. Above all, it will distill the company's own product development and production processes, corporate culture and business models into learnable and teachable concepts that are regularly updated and re-analyzed, thereby codifying the processes and original thinking that sets the organization apart for future generations of its managers. (See also the case study in the ExpressExec guide *Global Training and Development.*)

TAILORED DEGREES IN PRACTICE

It is difficult to cite good practice from a firm that has now ceased to exist because of its role in a major corporate scandal. The speed with which the top accountancy firm Arthur Andersen has fallen from grace in the wake of auditing omissions in the financial reporting of its client Enron is rightly sobering. But it is also a pity from the point of view of this guide because prior to the crisis it had pioneered one of the most successful in-company MBA programs on either side of the Atlantic – one which still provides a model for others to follow.

The training partner who opted for the program in 1997, Andrew Pawley, knew a great deal about MBAs. At the time he was in the final year of study for a part-time executive MBA program at London Business School and his wife had just graduated at the same school's full-time program. He reviewed the options available to Arthur Andersen and didn't like any of them.

Placing the professional staff on a conventional full-time program was impractical. The demands of working at Arthur Andersen would conflict with full-time study. If the firm chose one school, it would have trouble fitting in the numbers – Arthur Andersen wanted to place 50 alone in the first year – and if the people were spread out in different schools, they would lose the cohesion of a professional group and would be taught using different approaches.

From Pawley's perspective, consortium programs were also out. He felt Arthur Andersen's staff would not benefit from exposure to participants from a mixed group of companies because the exercise was linked to helping staff acquire a set of competencies that were specific to a professional services firm and there would be significant conflicts of interest if he attempted to set up a consortium made up of competitor firms. Yet he also felt that they would gain little from an in-company program – an MBA for accountants.

The solution he hit on was an initiative with two schools, Manchester and Warwick, which would provide professional staff with a full-blown MBA degree from one or other of the schools while enabling him to maintain a degree of input over how they are taught.

Arthur Andersen students studied for the MBA part-time over four years. They spent the first two years together at either Warwick or Manchester as a single stream or class, studying the business schools' compulsory core subjects. In years three and four, they joined the mainstream of the open MBA and selected options from the wide spectrum of electives offered by both of the schools. During this period they selected electives from either school and studied with other students. At the end, they were awarded an MBA from the school where the compulsory core subjects were studied.

The design adopted by Pawley meant that, to use a common English idiom, he could have his cake and eat it. The modular structure of the program did not lose the firm their staff for long periods, thus minimizing the disruption for its clients. Participants attended the business schools in five blocks of four days each year, from Wednesday to Saturday, and the timing of these blocks was structured so that students could integrate their managerial roles and responsibilities and balance these effectively with their personal life. It also meant that after each study block students could immediately apply and test what they learned back at the office.

In addition, the fact that Arthur Andersen staff studied for the core curriculum *en bloc* gave Pawley the cohesion and critical mass to support their learning as a group on site and more importantly back in the office while the ability of students to choose freely from the electives from both schools gave them a broader perspective, in terms of both subject matter and exposure to students from different industries, than they would have got on any one single program offered by another school.

To summarize, Arthur Andersen staff studied for the open modular MBA program at either Warwick or Manchester. The choice was up to the individual. Most of the staff from the firm's Northern and Scottish practices opted to study at Manchester, most from the Midlands practices at Warwick and the choice of school was evenly spread among staff from the South East. Pawley worked with academic staff from both institutions to tailor the program in four ways:

» the timing of the study – a Wednesday to Saturday study block meant that the firm only lost its staff for 12 working days a year;
» a focus on case studies drawn from sectors that Arthur Andersen were currently targeting;
» a modification of the basic finance module on the core program in the case of qualified accountants – although Pawley was keen to stress that no similar exemptions would be granted to staff from other specialist functions (for example human resources or marketing); and
» the inclusion of Arthur Andersen experts, clients and contacts as guest speakers on the program (for example, on derivatives management).

The issue that worried Pawley the most – that large numbers of Arthur Andersen students would swamp the program – did not prove a problem to the schools. "Their people are entering an already large pool," says Francesca Coles, Director of Executive MBAs at Warwick Business School at the time. "They study as a group for the core program. The electives are open to all our other students, regardless of how they are studying the program. These include 1,500 on the distance learning programs and over 200 on the part-time program. We can handle an extra 30 or even 50 students from the same company provided they are spread evenly and we avoid too high a concentration of AA staff in any one session. Because we run the same electives up to three times a year, this should not be a problem."

This was just as well, because the Arthur Andersen initiative looked set to become the largest of its kind in Europe. Following launches at each of the firm's offices in 1997, backed up by brochures and presentations from the deans of the two schools, 28 of Arthur Andersen's staff signed up to study at Manchester and 25 at Warwick. In 1998 the initiative was extended to administrative staff and professional staff not just from the assurance and business advisory practice but those covering tax, corporate finance and members of staff from their associated legal firms. Pawley was also piloting the scheme outside the UK. Of the 72 staff that started their studies in October 1998, six were from Paris, two from Spain, two from Belgium, one from Switzerland and one from Holland. In 1999, Pawley aimed to extend the scheme across Europe and increase the number of places to 100.

The Arthur Andersen initiative showed that tailoring can be undertaken in a way that does not compromise the basic principles of

Table 7.1 Tailored degrees: The pros and cons.

Pros	Cons
Immediate payback for the organization	Heavy on resources to launch and sustain
Strong focus on its industry and opportunity to use the organization's senior and line specialists as guest faculty	Limited perspective – excessive industry focus may undermine the benefit of general management education
Can be used by multisite and multinational organizations as a means of creating a cross-functional cross-cultural senior management team, thus meeting the organization's needs for the future	Lack of exposure to students outside the organization or industry may result in an excessively homogeneous corporate mindset
Golden handcuffs (students will remain with the organization during the program and this can be anchored by a loyalty contract)	Golden passport (if the degree has credibility in the external market – see Arthur Andersen MBA initiative above – staff may want to leave if their heightened career ambitions are not met (see Chapter 7))
Motivates staff by giving them an qualification accredited by an external academic institution	Value to the individual limited if the degree has little validity in the external labor market

MBA education. "The desire not to have a fully tailored MBA went right through the whole company," Pawley concluded. "Our senior staff were clear that it was in no one's interests to have an Andersen MBA. We would not benefit from the breadth of perspective our staff needed to do their work effectively and they would not benefit from a recognized and transferable general management qualification." (See Table 7.1.)

CONSORTIUM PROGRAMS IN PRACTICE

For those companies unwilling or unable to invest the resources required to set up an in-company learning center, consortium programs have been seen as the next best thing. The rationale for consortium programs was set out by Peter Lorange and Xavier Gilbert of the international school IMD in Lausanne, who concluded in 1998 that the relationship between schools and their clients needed a total overhaul.

"Schools will need to follow a consulting firm's way of operating," they say. "But while consulting firms have also performed high quality research on critical issues, and while their raison d'être is often to help bridge the gap between strategic priorities and specific behaviors, the distinctive competence of business schools should be in engineering executive learning. There must also be an underlying network of relationships, primarily between each firm and a business school but also among partners in consortia, leading to genuine learning networks."

Cosying up

The kind of network Lorange and Gilbert had in mind had been pioneered nearly a decade before by London's City University Business School. A "shadow" board was set up between founding members of the consortium – American Express, the International Stock Exchange, Sainsbury and the then government-owned Training Commission – which exercised control over the fees, syllabus and development of the program.

To provide a greater diversity of students, students from organizations were accepted onto the program. These organizations had associate member status and were not represented on the consortium board. They included Cadbury, Merill Lynch, British Telecom, Security

Pacific, Hoare Govett, Swallow Hotels, Chemunex, Hackney Health Authority, Tektronics and Honeywell Bull.

In its original form, the program had no fixed duration and no set syllabus. It centered not on the school but on the workplace of the MBA students. They decided, in conjunction with the company's internal HR practitioners, what course content would be most relevant to themselves and to their employers.

Tutors of the business school worked with each student to develop an individual program of learning, guiding participants through a series of company-based projects and other learning activities, with their managerial competence assessed jointly by company management, external academics and business school staff.

Students were able to select courses outside the business school, provided by consortium companies and by other centers of business education. Most importantly, students were assessed on the basis of their performance and not through written examinations.

No lectures? No GMAT test? *No written examinations?* The proposal presented the university authorities with a great deal to swallow and as the consortium representative selected as deputy director of the program explained, they needed a lot of convincing:

"The whole idea was that you would get people working how they knew best in an organizational context learning from workplace activities. The process of learning was continuously assessed by the university and relevantly trained people in the organizations. Teams of supervisors with senior status were trained in assessment and management of learning skills.

"In addition, bearing in mind that most of the students did not have a first degree and were judged as suitable on their track record, we developed a tool to identify the gaps in their knowledge and skills. We used the five core subjects of the University's full time MBA as a benchmark and piloted it among traditional MBA students. Many of these students told us that they preferred this method to the one they had completed for their conventional degree because it provided a measure not only of the knowledge gaps in terms of the academic disciplines – marketing, finance and organization etc. – but also the gaps in terms of their management skills.

"Finally, the workplace based assignments that were designed to substitute for a written examination had to be chosen at the highest level against criteria agreed by the university and the consortium board. We had to demonstrate to the university how these projects would be selected, conducted and assessed internally and the project had to be something really significant."

The methods pioneered by the Management MBA at City University have provided a model for many subsequent consortium programs. The University of Hong Kong, for example, ran a successful program in the early 1990s with a consortium of employers including Cathay Pacific Airways, HSBC and the Hong Kong Docks Authority. The students, who all lacked a first degree, undertook a foundation diploma and the most promising went on to take an MBA. The scheme was prompted by a lack of university places in the 1980s, which had resulted in many school leavers entering employment without having been given the opportunity to take a first degree.

In an initiative aimed at more senior managers, leading retailer Marks & Spencer approached London Business School in 1992 with a proposal for a consortium program involving a number of leading organizations in non-competing sectors. Jointly designing the program with LBS, M&S teamed up with the school to find other partners.

The resulting program "The Consortium for Executive Development" recruited British Airways, British Telecom, TSB, and Vauxhall Motors as partners. The program aims to broaden the perspective of executives whose exceptional performance has been achieved within their own organization. In practical terms, this is achieved by creating an environment in which individuals can benchmark on a number of important issues that affect all members and to make comparisons across organizations which will result in insight and solutions that aid them all.

"In Marks & Spencer, many executive-level managers had no experience of another company and we were struck how this was mirrored in many of the other companies we approached," says Helen Gates, management development training manager at M&S. "One of the great things about the program is that participants really get under the skins of the company and this is where the real learning begins."

Each corporate member of the program nominates five executives to take part in the program. The resulting group meets approximately once a month, with modules running typically for two and a half days, from early morning on the Wednesday of the relevant week until lunchtime. Each module covers a particular theme and is hosted by one of the consortium members.

During the first six months of 1998, consortium members have discussed issues as varied as managing new suppliers, new products and innovation, developing future leaders and managing people to create a better customer focus. "On completing the program, participants have a 'big picture' view of these themes and an appreciation of how they are handled in other top-flight organizations," says Helen Gates. "They will also have had the opportunity to build up a widely based network across a number of organizations which complements the in-company network in which they currently function.

"Most important of all, they will have had the opportunity to re-evaluate the standards they set for themselves and for other executives in the organization," she concludes. "As a consequence, they should emerge with a broader and deeper sense of the leadership role which top managers should play in leading business organizations."

KEY INSIGHTS

» Corporate universities differ from conventional corporate training centers in that they not only provide growth and development to the company's managers but act as the guardian and laboratory for the values and internal learning they develop. Specifically, they capture, distill and codify best practices, change management methods and firm-specific concepts, ensuring that these are kept up to date and disseminated across the board (Concord, General Electric, NatWest).

» Tailored degrees, developed in partnership with leading university business schools or independent management centers, perform a similar purpose. The learning is usually confined to a smaller management cadre, but it provides the individual participant with a bigger payback. The key challenge, not always achieved, is to integrate general management modules from the institution's open degree programs with firm-specific modules that explore how the concepts and good practice acquired can be applied in the organization's own sector or circumstances. Lack of exposure to students outside the organization or industry may result in an excessively homogenous corporate mindset. The value to the individual will also be limited if the degree has little validity in the external labor market (Arthur Andersen).

» One solution is to design and resource the degree in partnership with a consortium of other employers.

Key Concepts and Thinkers

» Competencies and needs analysis
» Appraisal and career management
» How organizations learn

Management development spans a number of common fields of research, depending on the focus and context of the specific initiative. Some of these, like teamwork and leadership, are covered in more detail in other ExpressExec titles. However, we have focused our attention on how concepts in these fields influence and affect the design and implementation of programs and courses in practice rather than covering the topic from a theoretical standpoint.

COMPETENCIES AND NEEDS ANALYSIS

The idea that the capabilities of both individuals and organizations – encompassing behaviors and values as well as skills and knowledge – provide firms with their key competitive resource emerged out of the soul searching that took place on both sides of the Atlantic in the late 1980s about the ability of companies to cope with radical change.

In the UK, independent researchers **Chris Hayes** and **Nickie Fonda** wrote a report, published by the government, called *Competence and Competition*. An important point of principle established by the report was that managers were increasingly being seen *collectively* as the key resource that influences the potential of the firm as a whole to respond to threats, exploit opportunities and change direction.

Know how and know what

In these new circumstances, argued Hayes and Fonda, the management development function's prime focus should not just be to develop managers capable of implementing the firm's current strategy but in identifying and responding to its future needs. This can be done using a variety of methods.

» *The scenario*: Sketching out the environment of the organization in 5–10 years time and the likely pressures on managers that result.
» *Critical success factors*: Key aspects of the overall business philosophy and strategy over the next few years are made explicit (possibly through a mission statement), key performance indicators are identified and the critical contributions of managers, and thus key management attributes, are drawn from these.
» *The human resource approach*: Companies with a long track record of successful performance are investigated for the attributes of their

managers that may have contributed to their success, with commonly occurring attributes imported into the investigating firm.

» *The learning needs approach*: The environment is scanned for potential future demands on managers, for example the impact of emerging information technology, and together with other organizations, the likely management attributes and competencies are built into a role description.

» *The strategic competence assessment*: The performance of units and departments is reviewed not only in terms of performance against plans and targets, but also in relation to the organization's ability to deal with unanticipated change.

All of these approaches, conclude Hayes and Fonda, bring the advantage that they attempt to "position" an organization's managers to cope with a changing environment. They are therefore not limited by its current plans. But their weaknesses are that they depend heavily on the quality of the conclusions being drawn and these are unlikely to be definitive. New and unanticipated needs generally emerge over time. Even though the analysis undertaken looks to the medium and long term, they must be reviewed frequently.

Hayes and Fonda, little known outside their own country, anticipated by five years the conclusions of the world renowned research of **Gary Hamel** and **C.K. Prahalad** on strategic core competencies – first published in classic fashion in a landmark article in *Harvard Business Review* in July 1994. Hamel and Prahalad explored the concept and outcomes of strategic competence assessment in more detail, stressing that managers needed to look much farther into the future of the business than they had been accustomed to.

The implications of the research on strategy development and innovation are explored in more depth in other ExpressExec titles, most notably *Strategy* and *The Innovative Individual*. But the lessons for management development are essentially the same as those advocated in *Competence and Competition*: any organization should ask itself two sets of questions about its business or activities under the headings "Today" and "In the Future," covering how they serve customers and by which channels, where competition stems from and what is the basis of the firm's competitive advantage; and from the responses, assess what skills and capabilities make the firm unique, both today and in the future.

The start point of both the Hayes/Fonda and Hamel/Prahalad approach to competence assessment is that the evaluation of essential management skills stems from the specific capabilities or potential of each organization, rather than a generic definition or framework. The reason this is so important was highlighted vividly in a research program by Dr **Wendy Hirsh** of the UK Institute for Employment Studies called *What Makes a Manager?* (see Chapter 2).

Hirsh's work established clearly that there is no universally transferable definition of management excellence; and that the difference between one and another lies not in the words used to describe the key competencies but in the organizational context that gives these words meaning.

A survey of 40 leading international corporations by Hirsh found that respondents expressed these competencies using a common vocabulary that included words like communication, leadership, judgment, initiative, organizing and motivation. But when these words are examined in the context of the perception and assumptions made by individual organizations, they lose their common meaning. "Good decision making," for example, means "taking innovative decisions" in one company and "analyzing hard data and minimizing commercial risk" in another.

Using this language as a means of assessing and developing managers, Hirsh argued, is effective only if there is a shared understanding of what this language means. "Managers use skills languages of their own all over the organization to take decisions about themselves and their subordinates," she says. "These decisions only achieve an acceptable degree of consistency if all managers thoroughly understand and share the real meaning of the language used. This places obvious constraints on the number of criteria that can be handled when drawing up ideal role descriptions. It also rules out the use of personnel jargon that is neither acceptable nor comprehensible."

Other academics and consultants have picked off specific functions, roles or sectors for their own approach to strategic competence assessment. Cranfield School of Management's Professor **Andrew Kakabadse** undertook a five-year research program in the early 1990s examining the capabilities of 7,500 senior executives in a variety of countries in Europe and Asia.

Among the generic competencies he identified were:

» *individual and collective insight*: not a hazy view of the future but a clear, down to earth pragmatic analysis concerning the position of suppliers and distributors, and an accurate appraisal of the current state of health of the organization;
» *a high quality of collective interaction and dialogue*, underpinned by *respect for each other and a sense of maturity*: this is explored in more depth in the section on team working below;
» *the ability to generate organizational targets and structures* that are not only meaningful to managers in the company but focus on attaining key business targets; and
» *the ability to communicate*: covering anything from policies and strategies to values and missions.

Similarly **Marsha Sinetar** of the Massachusetts Institute of Technology pinpointed the competencies of effective "intrepreneurs" (entrepreneurs working for large organizations) in 1988. She found that an ability to ask novel or disturbing questions, come up with unusual solutions and make innovations in the way their work gets done was central to all intrepreneurs and rules or cultural constraints that undermined these capabilities would render them not only useless but a menace to other people's work.

APPRAISAL AND CAREER MANAGEMENT

Career management was once the crown jewel of the HR practitioner's art. Spotting young management talent early and charting carefully woven tracks through the organizational maze so that they reached positions of strategic importance in sufficient time for them to make a real difference was the one aspect of personnel practice that cut real ice with the chief executive.

The fact that what was once called fast-track development would not be fast or flexible enough to anticipate changes on the scale that was hitting global business in the post-industrial age was spotted early on in the United States by Harvard Business School's Professor **Rosabeth Moss Kanter**.

In her first book *Men and Women of the Corporation*, she argues that radical changes would be needed to career management and appraisal to ensure that a more diverse range of candidates were considered for management posts, such as women and hitherto powerless individuals like clerical workers; and that intermediate jobs would need to be created to act as a bridge between clerical and management positions.

Backwards and forwards

The broad thrust of Moss Kanter's argument was explored in more depth in the UK by a trio of academics: Dr **Wendy Hirsh** of the Institute for Employment Studies, Professor **Lynda Gratton** of London Business School and **Val Hammond**, chief executive of Roffey Park Management Institute.

Hirsh focused on two failings in traditional fast-track development: the "halo" effect that results in a homogenous senior management team better able to deal with yesterday's problems rather than the challenges of tomorrow; and the elitist shortcomings of focusing too much time on a small cadre of "princes" at the expense of the broader management workforce. Her conclusions are explored in more detail in Chapter 2.

Gratton focuses more on the detailed mechanics. In a paper published in 1991, she argued that to survive at all, fast-track career schemes would have to:

» focus more consciously and faster on the immediate needs of the business: for example by sacrificing general management capabilities achieved through years of cross-business postings for business specific skills developed over a shorter period of time;

» compensate for the diminishing opportunity for lifetime careers in a single organization by opening up opportunities for workers of all ages, a move made possible by the shorter development time and promotion paths; and, at the same time

» design a more individual-centered system of appraisal which would ensure that clear and honest signals about the organization's and the employee's intentions were flushed out as soon as fast-changing economic or personal circumstances influenced them.

Val Hammond, in her early research work on developing women managers at Ashridge Management College, created the work–life agenda that was explored more fully in numerous flexible working initiatives in the 1990s and by a major UK government initiative at the turn of the millennium.

This agenda included:

» ensuring that women have training and particularly development throughout their careers in management;
» giving attention to career and life management for women;
» dealing with attitudes, assumptions and unfair practices that impede women's careers.

Of course, in pointing out the shortcomings of rigid, elitist career management practices to women, Hammond (and by implication Moss Kanter, Hirsh and Gratton) were also pointing out its shortcomings to all but a small minority of men. Many of the measures advocated by Hammond solely to tackle the effective development of women – creating a more diverse pool of talent to choose from, providing flexible entry and exit points on career paths and training in transferable skills – are now recognized as essential features of all career management strategies.

HOW ORGANIZATIONS LEARN

The impact of new concepts of organizational learning on both the strategy and tactics of developing managers has been immense. Prior to the idea that there were means for the workforce to engage in a systematic exchange of knowledge, ideas and good practice – both internally and with suppliers, distributors and alliance partners – training initiatives were a one-way process of inculcation and testing. What participants took away with them from syndicate discussions and project assignments was much more important to the sponsoring organization than what insights or understanding it gained itself.

Now the real focus is not on the input but the output. The origins of this turnaround lay in the theories of systems thinking advocated by **Peter Senge**, director of the Center of Organizational Learning at Massachusetts Institute of Technology. In his 1990 book *The Fifth Discipline*, Senge argued that an organization's ability to assimilate the information and insights it needs to keep abreast of rapid change lay in four "disciplines" that collectively provide the foundation for a fifth: systems thinking. These are:

» *personal mastery*: the principle of continuous, lifelong learning by the individual, "expanding the ability to produce the results we truly want in life;"
» *mental models*: uncovering and challenging those assumptions and mindsets that govern the individual's attitude to the world;
» *building shared vision*: creating "pictures of the future" that bring people together in pursuit of a common goal; and
» *team learning*: thinking and learning together as a group for more effective performance; this also enables members of the team to develop better than they would individually.

All of these disciplines, according to Senge, are interrelated. As he explains in *The Fifth Discipline*: "If people do not share a common vision, and do not share common 'mental models' about the business reality within which they operate, empowering people will only increase organizational stress and the burden of management to maintain coherence and direction."

Bodily functions

Most of the management development initiatives described in this ExpressExec title, including the case of Marks & Spencer with which we started the book, are heavily influenced by Senge's concept of systems thinking. Training needs analysis is used to pinpoint and highlight the contrasts between the assumptions and mindsets that govern individual managers' and the organization's vision of the world. A combination of pre-program assignments and plenary or syndicate discussions focused on a single topic help to create a common goal or mental map, reinforced by team learning.

A good example is a series of programs designed and conducted by **John Stopford** of London Business School in 1997 for the pharmaceutical giant Glaxo Wellcome (now GlaxoSmithKline). Stopford argues that the confidence managers have in themselves, their company and their role in the company has a direct bearing on their ability to develop ways of thinking that lead to innovative solutions.

In an event designed to promote a shared view of the future among the 300 most senior managers of the corporation, the whole of the second week, conducted at the Fuqua Business School at Duke University in South Carolina, focused on each individual manager, the kind of company he or she wants to build and what part he or she will have in building it.

In companies like GlaxoSmithKline, many people are in senior positions because of their specialist skills. Part of the aim of the program, Stopford says, was to help them quantify the corporate and industrial understanding they sometimes do not realize they have. The course curriculum, he adds, can be summed up as: "How does the company work, and how does it work for you guys?". It recognizes that modern corporations are built on the confidence senior managers have in each other and discusses what this means and how it changes their behavior.

How individuals and teams learn

Peter Senge's thinking on the mindsets that people hold about their work and organization was deeply influenced by Harvard Business School professor **Chris Argyris**'s seminal work on how individuals learn.

Argyris starts from the premise that each individual has a potential that can be developed – or stultified – by the environment and circumstances in which he or she works. In an article for *Harvard Business Review* in 1991, he studied six companies and observed 265 decision-making meetings. He concluded that executive behavior often creates an atmosphere of distrust and inflexibility, despite the fact that the managers involved genuinely believe trust and innovation to be crucial to good decision-making. This pattern of behavior was not confined to businesses, extending to managers operating in government, trade unions, the church and other non-profit sectors.

Argyris's solution is for both individuals and team to test what assumptions and conclusions have been drawn in collective discussions by seeking feedback about their own and each other's behavior during "quiet and non-risky" times. In this way they create a second or "double" loop of learning, acting on the feedback they receive to break down defensive behavior which, according to Argyris, "is self-perpetuating because they learn nothing but the importance of conforming."

Learning together on your own

Argyris's concept of double loop learning transformed both the design and importance of plenary and syndicate work in management development initiatives. It shifted the focus from what is said on courses and seminars – by experts, organizers and guest speakers – to what has been understood and assimilated by participants. Syndicate and plenary assignments designed to promote shared discussion and learning provides the focus for the second loop of learning, promoting a synergistic pool of insights and conclusions that not only breaks down defensive behavior in individuals but a resource that the organization can draw on.

Double loop learning also helped to rehabilitate the theories of the British advocate of action learning **Reg Revans**. Revans' start point – that managers learn better in practical working situations than they ever could in a classroom – was first formulated in the 1930s where he was responsible for technical and professional education for a county council in East England. It took nearly five decades to take hold, leaving Revans bitter and defensive about the lack of recognition he received in his own country.

Yet the basic principle of action learning – that understanding and insight arise out of practical experience rather than preceding it – underpins the learning strategies adopted in virtually all outdoor learning programs, crisis management exercises and scenario-based assignments.

A senior manager taking part in a series of action learning "sets" covering change management, project management and performance management in the UK Civil Service described it like being "continually woken up by an alarm clock." Revans may have found it hard to build action learning into an all-encompassing management concept but every HR practitioner or trainer designing practical assignments for a management course owes him an incalculable debt.

KEY LEARNING POINTS

» Linking management development initiatives to strategic goals can be achieved in a number of ways. The most common are based on scenario-based projections of the future, an assessment of critical success factors, an assessment of the human resource capabilities of the organization, and an assessment of the likely future skills and capabilities that will be needed by key professional staff.

» All of these approaches bring the advantage that they attempt to "position" an organization's managers to cope with a changing environment. They are therefore not limited by its current plans. But their weaknesses are that they depend heavily on the quality of the conclusions being drawn and these are unlikely to be definitive. New and unanticipated needs generally emerge over time. Even though the analysis undertaken looks to the medium and long term, they must be reviewed frequently (Fonda/Hayes).

» Two failings in traditional fast-track development are the "halo" effect that results in a homogeneous senior management team better able to deal with yesterday's problems rather than the challenges of tomorrow; and the elitist shortcomings of focusing too much time on a small cadre of "princes" at the expense of the broader management workforce (Hirsh).

» To compensate, fast-track career schemes need to focus more consciously and faster on the immediate needs of the business; compensate for the diminishing opportunity for lifetime careers in a single organization by opening up opportunities for workers of all ages, a move made possible by the shorter development time and promotion paths; and at the same time design a more individual-centered system of appraisal which would ensure that clear and honest signals about the organization's and the employee's intentions were flushed out as soon as fast-changing economic or personal circumstances influence them (Gratton).

» Executive behavior often creates an atmosphere of distrust and inflexibility, despite the fact that the managers involved genuinely believe trust and innovation to be a crucial to good decision-making. The solution is for both individuals and team to test what assumptions and conclusions have been drawn in collective discussions by seeking feedback about their own and each other's behavior during "quiet and non-risky" times. In this way they create a second or "double" loop of learning, acting on the feedback they receive to break down defensive behavior (Argyris).

» The basic principle of action learning – that understanding and insight arise out of practical experience rather than preceding it – underpins the learning strategies adopted in virtually all outdoor learning programs, crisis management exercises and scenario-based assignments (Revans).

Resources

- » Books
- » E-learning providers
- » List of addresses

This chapter lists books, articles and Websites that you may find useful in furthering your study of boardroom education. Some related publications are listed in chapter 9 of the ExpressExec titles *Boardroom Education* and *Global Training and Development*.

BOOKS

» Mumford, A. 1997 *Management Development: Strategies for Action*. IPD Books (UK), London.

Alan Mumford is the UK's foremost expert on management development. This book is predicated on his main premise. This is that "informal" management development, where learning is drawn directly from the job, is only effective if it forms part of an integrated strategy where goals and outcomes balance the personal needs of the individual with the commercial needs of the organization. The chapter on creating the right learning environment is particularly good.

» Fee, K. 2001 *A Guide to Management Development Techniques*. Kogan Page, London.

This starts off with a comprehensive chapter on how managers learn, covering experiential and informal learning as well as the formal assimilation of knowledge and skills. The framework developed by Fee to encompass and integrate these forms of learning is the book's most valuable transferable asset. The e-learning chapter, covering many of the issues raised in Chapter 4 in this book, is far more up to date than in other standard guides.

» Woodall, J. and Winstanley, D. 1998 *Management Development: Strategy and Practice*. Blackwell Business Books, Oxford.

Woodall and Winstanley are from Kingston Business School and Imperial Management School, two of the most cutting edge newcomers to the UK's business education industry in the last decade. The early chapters cover much of the same ground as the two basic guides above, but their book really comes into its own towards the end when the authors cover in some detail the specific needs of particular types of manager – most importantly women, the top team, international managers and professionals. Well worth getting just for this section alone.

» Burgoyne, J. and Reynolds, M. (eds) 1997 *Management Learning: Integrating Perspectives in Theory and Practice*. Sage, London.

Burgoyne is to learning what Mumford (see above) is to management development. This rather academic tome, like most edited books, is a curate's egg. Worth getting for the contributions by Richard Bolt and Michael Reynolds on how learning applies to groups and the design of groupwork; management learning as a discourse by Norman Fairclough and Ginny Handy; and action learning by Mike Pedlar, a pioneer of self-development in the 1980s. Others chapters are hard work.

» Handy, C., Gordon, C., Gow, I., and Randlesomme, C. 1988 *Making Managers*. Pitman, London.

Well out of date in both its findings and perspectives, this book – based on the findings of the seminal Handy report – compares the training and performance of managers in the United States, Japan, France, West Germany and Great Britain. All the authors are British academics and the conclusions were used to reform (not very successfully) the framework governing UK business education. That said, the measures and diagnostic tools used to make the comparisons are still applicable today and the book is a still a useful grounder for anyone developing an international management development strategy (see ExpressExec guide *Global Training and Development*).

» Hunt, J. and Weintraub, J. 2002 *The Coaching Manager*. Sage Publications, California/London.

Hot off the press at the time of this guide going to print is this detailed guide by two expert academics at Babson College in the United States. The book starts by distinguishing between mentoring and coaching and setting the basic principles of coaching in the context of Daniel Goleman's theories of emotional intelligence (see chapter 8 of the ExpressExec guide *The Innovative Individual*). The model advocated by the authors covers elements such as creating the right environment, assessing who is and isn't "coachable," focusing on what is important, observing without inferring, providing balanced feedback and setting goals. Hunt and Weintraub cover each of these in turn, using anonymized examples drawn from their own experience. They then pioneer the concept of "the coaching manager," looking at how this key role can be used at all levels of the organization.

E-LEARNING PROVIDERS

Note: The descriptions are taken from the organizations' Websites.

» AthenaOnline (US Institute for Management Studies) http://www.thenewleader.com

"AthenaOnline is a premier publisher of multimedia training, education and career development products. We are an Internet 'knowledge network' headquartered in the San Francisco Bay Area, California."

» Caliber Learning Network http://www.caliberlearning.com

"Caliber is the world's leading developer and distributor of Internet-based training and business communication solutions to corporations and institutions."

» Centra http://www.centra.com

"Web-based software and services for live collaboration, enabling business interaction, collaborative commerce and corporate learning."

» click2learn.com http://www.click2learn.com

"A leader provider of full service e-learning solutions to businesses, government agencies and educational institutions throughout the world."

» Corporate University X-Change http://www.corpu.com

"A corporate education research and consulting firm that assists organizations in optimizing their learning resources."

» DigitalThink http://www.digitalthink.com

"DigitalThink is the leader in designing, developing and deploying e-learning solutions to Fortune 1000 companies."

» Docent http://.www.docent.com

"Docent is a provider of e-learning products and services that enable the Web-based exchange of personalized and measurable knowledge within and among large enterprises, education content providers and professional communities."

» Eduventures.com http://www.eduventures.com

"Eduventures.com Inc is a provider of education technology industry analysis, market data and insight to buyers, suppliers and users of e-learning products and services."

» Executive Development Associates http://www.executivedevelopment.com

"Executive Development Associates (EDA) is a leading education and consulting firm specializing in the strategic use of executive/leadership development."

» Forum Corporation http://www.forum.com

"A global leader in workplace learning ... pioneering new ways to achieve business results through learning. We specialize in creating innovative solutions that help companies build competitive advantage and lasting customer loyalty."

» FT Knowledge http://.www.ftknowledge.com

"FT Knowledge is one of the world's leading providers of business education and management development. We specialize in providing learning and development that is highly relevant to the needs of business and those who work within it."

» Institute for Management Studies http://www.ims-online.com

"A leader in executive education and management development for over 25 years, IMS holds one-day workshops on cutting edge management issues, taught by leading business school professors from the graduate schools at Harvard, University of Pennsylvania, UC Berkeley, Penn State, Stanford, SMU, Georgetown and others."

» Knowledge Universe (KU) http://www.knowledgeu.com

"Knowledge Universe (KU) operates, incubates and invests in leading companies that build human capital by helping organizations and individuals to realize their full potential."

» Parthenon Group http://www.parthenon.com

"The Parthenon Group ... provide[s] strategic advisory consulting services to business leaders who demand seasoned counsel and seek true business insights that yield results."

» Pensare http://www.pensare.com

"Pensare develops Knowledge Community online learning solutions that drive teamwork, creativity and business results through the innovative use of strategic alliances, validated content, leading technology, applied learning tools, human interaction and cultural adaptation."

» Provant http://www.provant.com

"We provide integrated solutions that resolve performance-based organizational challenges."

» Quisic http://www.quisic.com

"Your freeline resource for the most current business thinking on the Web. Business education solutions for corporations and academic institutions."

» Saba http://www.saba.com

"Saba is a leading provider of e-learning infrastructure, which consists of Internet-based learning management systems, business to business learning exchanges and related services."

» SmartForce http://www.smartforce.com

"Smartforce is redefining learning for the Internet age with its first of a kind, fully integrated, Internet-based e-Learning technology."

» SMGnet-Strategic Management Group http://www.smgnet.net/homei.htm

"SMGnet, the online learning, development and delivery division of Strategic Management Group, Inc., concentrates on solving business issues by supporting the growth and development of human capital via the Internet."

» Tacit http://www.tacit.com

"Tacit Knowledge Systems, Inc., is a pioneer and leader in providing automated knowledge discovery and exchange systems that, for the first time, offers organizations automated access to explicit, tacit and even private knowledge."

» The Learning Partnership (TLP) http://www.tlp.org

"The Learning Partnership is owned by some of the world's leading business academies. Our mission is to create and share knowledge around the key issues facing business in the new Millennium."

» Unext http://www.unext.com

"Unext was created to deliver world class education. We are building a scalable education business that delivers the power of knowledge around the world."

Source: Al Vicere, Smeal College of Business Administration, 2000.

LIST OF ADDRESSES

American Assembly of Collegiate
Schools of Business
(AACSB)
600 Emerson Road, Suite 300
St Louis, MO 63141-6762
USA
Tel: +1 314-872-8481
Fax: +1 314-872-8495
Website: http://www.aacsb.edu

The Association of Business
Schools
344/354 Gray's Inn Road
London WC1X 8BP
Tel: +44 20 7837 1899
Fax: +44 20 7837 8189
E-mail: 106262.227@compuserve.
com
Website: http://www.leeds.ac.uk/
bes/abs/abshome.htm

Association for Management
Education and Development
14–15 Belgrave Square
London SW1X 8PS
Tel: +44 20 7235 3505
Fax: +44 20 7235 3565
E-mail: amed.office@anet.
demon.co.uk

Association of Management
Development
Institutions in South Asia
8-2-333/A Road No 3 Banjara Hill
Ind – Hyderabad 500034
India
Tel: +91 40 244089
Fax: +91 40 244801

The Anderson School at UCLA
110, Westwood Plaza
Box 951481
Los Angeles, CA 90095-1481
United States
Tel: +1 310-825-6944
Fax: +1 310-825-8582
Website: http://www.anderson.
ucla.edu

Ashridge Management College
Ashridge, Berkhamsted
Hertfordshire HP4 1NS
United Kingdom
Tel: +44 1442 841000
Fax: +44 1442 841306
E-mail: info@ashridge.org.uk

Association of MBAs
15 Duncan Terrace
London N1 8BZ
Tel: +44 20 7837 3375
Fax: +44 20 7278 3634

Berkeley – see Haas School of
Business

Business Association of Latin
American Studies
c/o School of Business
Administration
University of San Diego
5998 Alcala Park
San Diego, CA 92110
USA
Tel: +1 619-260-4836
Fax: +1 619-260-4891
E-mail: dimon@acusd.edu

Bocconi – see SDA Bocconi
University of Cambridge – Judge
Institute of Management Studies
Trumpington Street
Cambridge CB2 1AG
United Kingdom
Tel: +44 1223 337051/2/3
Fax: +44 1223 339581
Website: http://www.jims.cam.ac.
uk/mba

Centre for High Performance
Development
Elvetham Hall
Hartley Wintney
Hampshire RG27 8AS
United Kingdom
Tel: +44 1252 842677
Fax: +44 1252 842564
E-mail: info@chpd.co.uk

The Chinese University of Hong
Kong
Faculty of Business Administration
Leung Kau Kui Building
Shatin, New Territories
Hong Kong, PRC
Tel: +852 609 7642
Fax: +852 603 5762

Columbia Business School
Uris Hall, 3022 Broadway
New York, NY 10027
United States
Tel: +1 212-854-1961
Fax: +1 212-662-6754
Website: http://www.columbia.
edu

Central and East European
Management Development
Association
Brdo pri Kranju
4000 Kranj
Slovenia
Tel: +386 64 221–761
Fax: +386 64 222–070
E-mail: ceeman@iedc-brdo.si

China Europe International
Business School
Jiatong University, Minhang
Campus
800, Dong Chuan Road
Shanghai 200240,
People's Republic of China
Tel: +8621 6463 0200
Fax: +8621 6435 8928

City University Business School
Frobisher Crescent
Barbican Centre
London EC2Y 8HB
United Kingdom
E-mail: cubs-postgrad@city.ac.uk
Website:
http//www.city.ac.uk/cubs

Concord School of Management
194 Beacon Street
Chestnut Hill, MA 02467–3853
United States
Tel: +1 617-552-2877
Fax: +1 617-552-2051
E-mail: information@concordsom.
edu
Website: http://www.concord-
som.edu

Cranfield School of Management
Cranfield, Bedford MK43 0AL
United Kingdom
Tel: +44 1234 751122
Fax: +44 1234 751806
Website: http://www.cranfield@
ac.uk/som

European Foundation for
Management Development
88, rue Gachard
B-1050 Brussels
Belgium
Tel: +32 2 648 0385
Fax: +32 2 646 0768
E-mail: info@efmd.be
Website: http://www.efmd.be

Graduate Management Admission
Council (GMAC)
8300 Greensboro Drive Suite 750
Mclean, VA 22102
USA
Tel: +1 703-749-0131
Fax: +1 703-749-0169
E-mail: gmacmail@gmac.com
Website: http://www.gmat.org

Harvard Business School
Soldiers Field
Boston, MA 02163
United States
Tel: +1 617-495-6127
Fax: +1 617-496-9272
Website: http://www.hbs.edu

E.M. Lyon
23 avenue Guy de Collongue
BP 174, 69132 Ecully Cédex
France
Tel: +33 4 78 33 78 65
Fax: +33 4 78 33 61 69
Website: http://www.em-lyon.
com

European Institute for Advanced
Studies in Management
Rue d'Egmont 13
B-1000 Brussels
Belgium
Tel: +32 2 511 9116
Fax: +32 2 512 1929

Haas School of Business
University of California at Berkeley
S440 Student Services Building
No 1902
Berkeley, CA 94720-1902
United States
Tel: +1 510-642-1405
Fax: +1 510-643-6659
Website: http://www.haas.
berkeley.edu

HEC School of Management
1 rue de la Libération
78351 Jouy-en-Joas Cédex
France
Tel: +33 1 39 67 73 79/73 82
Fax: +33 1 39 67 74 65
Website: http://www.hec.fr

Henley Management College
Greenlands, Henley-on-Thames
Oxfordshire RG9 3AU
United Kingdom
Tel: +44 1491 571454
Fax: +44 1491 571635
E-mail: info@henley.co.uk
Website:
http://www.henleymc.ac.uk

Imperial College Management
School
53, Prince's Gate
Exhibition Road
London SW7 2PG
United Kingdom
Tel: +44 20 7594 9205
Fax: +44 20 7823 7685
E-mail: m.school@ic.ac.uk
Website: http://ms.ic.ac.uk

Institute of Personnel and
Development
IPD House, Camp Road
London SW19 4UX
Tel: +44 20 8971 9000

IMD (International Institute for
Management Development)
Chemin de Bellerive 23, PO Box
915
CH 1001 Lausanne, Switzerland
Tel: +41 21 618 0111
Fax: +41 21 618 0707
E-mail: info@imd.ch
Website: http://www.imd.ch

IESE – International Graduate
School of Management
University of Navarra
Avenida Pearson 21
08034 Barcelona
Spain
Tel: +34 93 253 4229
Fax: +34 93 253 4343
Website: http://www.iese.edu

Institute for Employment Studies
Mantell Building
University of Sussex
Brighton BN1 9RF
United Kingdom
Tel: +44 1273 686751
Fax: +44 1273 690430

INSEAD
Boulevard de Constance
77305 Fontainebleau Cédex
France
Tel: +33 1 60 72 40 00
Fax: +33 1 60 74 55 00
Website: http://www.insead.fr

Leonard N. Stern School of
Business
New York University
44 West 4th Street
New York, NY 10012-1126
United States
Tel: +1 212-998-0600
Fax: +1 212-995-4231
Website: http://www.stern.
nyu.edu

London Business School
Sussex Place, Regent's Park
London NW1 4SA
United Kingdom
Tel: +44 20 7262 5050
Fax: +44 20 7724 7875
Website: http://www.lbs.ac.uk

Manchester Business School
Booth Street West
Manchester M15 6PB
United Kingdom
Tel: +44 161 275 7139
Fax: +44 161 275 6556
Website: http://www.mbs.ac.uk

University of Michigan Business
School
701 Tappan Street
Ann Arbor, MI 48109-1234
United States
Tel: +1 734-763-5796
Fax: +1 734-763-7804
Website:
http://www.bus.umich.edu

The Open University Business
School
Walton Hall
Milton Keynes MK7 6AA
United Kingdom
Tel: +44 1908 653449
Fax: +44 1908 654320
Website: http://www.oubs.open.
ac.uk

Lyon – see E.M. Lyon

Massachusetts Institute of
Technology – see
MIT Sloan School of Management

MIT Sloan School of Management
Massachusetts Institute of
Technology
50 Memorial Drive
Cambridge, MA 02142
Tel: +1 617-253-3730
Fax: +1 617-253-6405
Website:
http://web.mit.edu/sloan/
www/

Roffey Park Management Institute
Forest Road, Horsham, West
Sussex
United Kingdom
Tel: +44 1293 851644
Fax: +44 1293 851565
E-mail: info@roffey-park.co.uk

Stanford Graduate School of
Business
Stanford University
Stanford, CA
United States
Tel: +1 650-723-2766
Fax: +1 650-725-7831
Website: http://gsb-www.stan-
ford.edu

SDA Bocconi
Masters Division
Via Balilla 16-18
20136 Milan
Italy
Tel: +39 2 58363281
Fax: +39 2 58363275
Website: http://www.sda.uni-bocconi.it

Stern - see Leonard N. Stern
School of Business

Sundridge Park Management
Centre
Plaistow Lane, Bromley
Kent BR1 3TP
United Kingdom
Tel: +44 20 8313 3131

Warwick Business School
University of Warwick
Coventry CV4 7AL
United Kingdom
Tel: +44 1203 523922
Fax: +44 1203 524643
Website: http://www.wbs.warwick.ac.uk

Strathclyde Graduate Business
School
199 Cathedral Street
Glasgow G4 0QU
United Kingdom
Tel: +44 141 553 6118/9
Fax: +44 141 552 8851
Website: http://www.strath.ac.uk/
Department/SGBS

UCLA - see The Anderson School
at UCLA

Wharton School
University of Pennsylvania
102 Vance Hall
3733 Spruce Street
Philadelphia, PA
United States
Tel: +1 215-898-6183
Fax: +1 215-898-0120
Website: http://www.wharton.upenn.edu

Ten Steps to Making it Work

1 Don't rely on generic definitions of management skills
2 Test every assumption you and your sponsoring managers make about the needs and expectations of participants
3 Choose suppliers that know your business
4 Create an environment that is both safe and challenging
5 Link the output of the assignments to clear learning objectives
6 Leave enough time for syndicate work – but keep it focused
7 Capture the results
8 Sustain the learning
9 Keep your talent pool wide and diverse
10 Be a good broker and consultant, not a jack of all trades

1. DON'T RELY ON GENERIC DEFINITIONS OF MANAGEMENT SKILLS

When drawing up definitions of the key skills and capabilities that will provide the start point for any management development initiative, factor in the way these are likely to be interpreted on the ground given the specific context in which they will be applied. Research by Wendy Hirsh at the UK Institute for Employment Studies and Johaan Roos at the Institute for Management Development in Lausanne (see Chapter 6) suggests that common terms like "effective decision making" and "good leadership" have radically different meanings from one sector, and even one organization, to another.

If you have not already done so, conduct a comprehensive organizational needs analysis that pinpoints not only the skills and capabilities managers need now, but those they are likely to require in 5–10 years' time. Also remember that initiatives that help to shape how managers think, see and think about their work and the world in which their organization operates are likely to be as important as those that shape what they do.

2. TEST EVERY ASSUMPTION YOU AND YOUR SPONSORING MANAGERS MAKE ABOUT THE NEEDS AND EXPECTATIONS OF PARTICIPANTS

Management development initiatives most commonly fail because participants and sponsors have different expectations about what each is going to get out of the exercise. Always conduct a training needs analysis exercise prior to the start that aims to position everyone – sponsors, organizers and participants – in a common start point. Bear in mind the most important conclusion made by *The Fifth Discipline's* Peter Senge (see Chapter 8) that if people do not share a common vision of where the organization is going or similar assumptions and mindsets about their work, any attempt to build on their capabilities will exacerbate existing divisions rather than heal them.

3. CHOOSE SUPPLIERS THAT KNOW YOUR BUSINESS

Whether you are commissioning an academic expert to make a formal presentation or a consultancy with a specialist approach to the task in hand, their ability to add value to the program will depend on how they tailor or position their expertise in the context of the specific needs of participants. This may involve working with you to develop firm-specific exercises, case material or scenarios as well as the capacity to see the world from the mindset of participants. Check their track record and seek references if necessary.

4. CREATE AN ENVIRONMENT THAT IS BOTH SAFE AND CHALLENGING

Sounds a contradiction, doesn't it? However, people are only able to *think* and *act* dangerously if they *feel* safe. There is a balance to maintain between lifting individuals out of their immediate working environment into one where their mental and physical horizons will be broadened; and one where their survival instincts – which kick in at different times in different people – will shut down their capacity to respond to any intellectual or empathetic challenge.

As the leading UK expert in outdoor development David Charlton stresses: "Outdoor providers who prescribe stress, threat and arbitrary challenge and who specialize in exposing individual weakness, abusing the client's vulnerability in the name of management development, are to be viewed with caution. They will at the very least leave people out of touch with each other and with themselves."

5. LINK THE OUTPUT OF THE ASSIGNMENTS TO CLEAR LEARNING OBJECTIVES

Well-crafted scenarios, team exercises or activity-based learning will result in very little other than a welcome day out for the participants unless the insights and capabilities they inspire are closely linked to the needs identified in the training needs analysis.

The emergency response exercise run for deputy department heads of the Hong Kong government (see Chapter 6) was not intended to test the crisis management skills of the participants. They and the sponsoring team at the Hong Kong Civil Service knew they already possessed these and the initial decisions taken collectively by the participants more than confirmed this.

The exercise was designed to test their ability to communicate and justify their decisions to a new set of stakeholders that included local politicians and recently launched newspapers and radio stations. Here the participants performed less well, not because their communication *skills* were poor (they presented well at simulated press conferences) but because their responses revealed a traditional "civil service" inability to accept that they had to justify their actions publicly and this was an essential part of the job.

The syndicate work that followed focused entirely on this attitude problem. The emphasis in the exercise – that success came from winning public support for the right decisions rather than taking them in the first place – pinpointed where future development activity was needed. A conventional crisis management simulation, however well designed and executed, would not have achieved this.

6. LEAVE ENOUGH TIME FOR SYNDICATE WORK – BUT KEEP IT FOCUSED

Syndicate work is the best opportunity you have for achieving what Harvard's Chris Argyris calls double loop learning (see Chapter 6): bedding down ideas and clarifying what implications and uses the new concepts or techniques have for the group. Our experience suggests, however, that too little time is devoted to syndicate work because it is regarded as an afterthought rather than the centerpiece of the initiative. Formal assignments are also needed to get the maximum benefit from the exercise. Participants need to be able to work with the concepts or try out the techniques rather than simply discuss them.

7. CAPTURE THE RESULTS

In an age when innovation is the new competitive imperative, any means to inspire and capture original thought is at a premium. The insights and conclusions that lie scrawled on flipchart sheets and whiteboards after an intense piece of syndicate or plenary work were once thought to be a by-product, a sign that participants were properly engaged in the learning process. They had little intrinsic value of their own. Now they are main output, the base material from which groundbreaking firm-specific concepts, services and products are shaped. Capturing and codifying this material – in newsletters, intranets or e-mail circulars – should be a first-step priority immediately after the formal program.

8. SUSTAIN THE LEARNING

Disseminating the material from the formal program is also important because it helps to sustain the learning. Successful syndicate and plenary work generates an energy and enthusiasm among participants that can prove an invaluable personal and organizational resource. But it quickly dissipates if close follow up contact is not maintained.

In the best initiatives, the formal program is the start, not the end point of the learning. The introduction of computer-based intranet, discussion database and brainstorming software opens up the possibility of semi-permanent learning groups forged during successful formal programs that will provide a continuous source of personal and organizational development.

Sponsored and encouraged by senior management support and drawing on their own concepts and insights drawn from the original program, these groups will provide the organization with the kind of amebic dynamism that will enable it to stay ahead of change.

9. KEEP YOUR TALENT POOL WIDE AND DIVERSE

Job for life is gone. Predicting talent needs is a game of poker, not bridge. The cards change each round, so should your response. Betting your organization's future on a small number of queens and kings is dangerous if your opponent has the right combination of lower cards.

Career management is still important but whatever strategy you develop should be flexible, incorporating multi-entry points and criteria that do not exclude candidates without the kind of halo that senior managers conventionally associate with success. The communication should also be open and two-way, particularly during periods of intense change like a merger or acquisition, so that you do not wind up losing your best people because of misunderstandings about their prospects.

Diversity is not simply a matter of equity. L'Oreal, the number one producer of beauty products since 1978, has founded its success on a steady stream of new products and a rapid expansion into Europe, the Americas and Asia during the 1990s.

The company now boasts 400 subsidiaries, 500 brands and representatives in 150 countries. It comprises four main cosmetics divisions: Salon; Consumer; Perfumes and Beauty; and Active Cosmetics. L'Oreal also operates in pharmaceuticals, dermatology and related fields, and it attaches a high priority to research activities leading to new product developments.

In these circumstances, the managers and the professionals it recruits are expected to have a solid body of expert knowledge about the properties of the product they are responsible for – and also the ability to tailor their sales approach to meet high localized needs.

In pursuit of this goal, the company's head office reflects the greatest possible mix of nationalities and backgrounds. For example, Louvet's own department includes the following: a 28-year old woman with an Oxford University degree in French and Latin; an Italian who studied music and then took a business course at the French business school HEC; an executive with dual Japanese and US nationalities; plus Portuguese, Greek and Vietnamese nationals.

10. BE A GOOD BROKER AND CONSULTANT, NOT A JACK OF ALL TRADES

In all but the smallest firms, HR practitioners are brokers and consultants in the management development process, championing the need for continuous development, identifying the right needs and choosing the methods and external suppliers needed to meet them.

Our own experience suggests that the best initiatives involve a close partnership between the organization's own management development or HR manager; and external suppliers who have valuable expertise but need to draw on the internal manager's own insider knowledge of the firm, its culture and the likely response of its managers to the intervention on offer.

It is a difficult balance to maintain. If the external suppliers are given too free a hand, the initiative will often fail to inspire the right response from participants because it is perceived as "off the shelf" and not geared to the organization's specific needs. If the internal HR practitioner exerts too great a control, they will not benefit from the supplier's broader knowledge of what techniques do and do not work in practice.

Frequently Asked Questions (FAQs)

Q1: Can you measure the benefits?

A: In objective terms, no. In subjective terms, yes. But it is the subjective terms that really count. As we explained in Chapter 2, this is all about influencing the way individuals think, see, and feel about their work and how the key stakeholders in their working lives – employees, colleagues, line managers, customers, and partners – see, think, and feel about them.

Since the criteria are a matter of subjective perception, measuring whether this perception has changed in the weeks and months after the initiative will give you a fairly accurate indication whether it has achieved the desired results. Big corporations have experimented with more objective criteria. Rank Xerox has identified an empirical link between long-term customer satisfaction and sustained employee satisfaction brought about, among other things, by systematic management development; but in the end we are still dealing with opinion rather than fact.

Q2: How many key functions can be done over the Net?

A: This is all about comfort with the medium. As we saw in Chapter 4, the more individuals feel able to exchange freely with colleagues through a computer screen in the way that they would face to face, the more syndicate work and collective learning assignments can be undertaken in this way.

At the moment, the consensus is that the foundation of what is now termed a "blended" management development initiative – in terms of charismatic delivery of expert knowledge and team bonding through the tacit language of a face to face encounter – needs the physical contact of a "direct" encounter. Once this bond has been established, everything else can be undertaken virtually. But in an age when people meet and get married over the Net, views about what constitutes "tacit" and "direct" are being transformed day by day. Watch this space.

Q3: Is career management still a viable HR function?

A: Yes, provided all the parties concerned – the individual, the HR practitioner, the line manager and the Board – are honest about the changing parameters of what constitutes a career. Rule 1 is that everything is subject to change. Individuals' expectations of what they want from a career change year by year, as do the economic circumstances that determine whether the organization can meet these expectations. As the commercial imperatives of the firm shift, so will the key capabilities they require of their managers.

Rule 2 is honesty in acknowledging that this is the case. The misunderstandings that lead to an organization losing the key managers it wants to keep usually occur because a lack of open feedback is prompting the individual to second guess his or her prospects. Most often this consists of checking out what is available elsewhere and if they start doing this there is a more than evens chance that they will find something worth moving for. This happens most frequently during a period of intense change brought about by, say, a merger or a new commercial alliance. Doubts about a future with the firm will spread like wildfire from the moment the first rumors hit the press. Honesty from day one is the best way of dousing the embers.

Q4: How can I convince potential sponsors that it needs to be done?

A: The need for continuous professional development is now so firmly established in principle in the minds of senior managers that it has become apple pie. In practice, the question to answer is "is this specific initiative worth the cost and time?" Even if you can convince potential sponsors of the theoretical need for the initiative, your carefully calculated assessment of what time and resources are required will be whittled down to the barest practical minimum.

Time is often more at stake than money. Releasing precious "human resources" for training is never popular with line managers. The three day residential course you envisaged may have to be pared down to an evening after a full working day plus the day after or a series of sessions held in between meetings in the company boardroom. As with all negotiations, you need to establish fall-back positions and a clear sense of where the bottom line output will be undermined.

On a crisis communications program, for example, the design originally called for the participants to take part in a two-day residential program. At the last minute, it had to be cut back to a single day. An essential feature of the program was that it should be run "real time" to reproduce the exact pressures of a real crisis. The crisis simulated occurred in the early hours of the morning, so the organizers agreed to the single day seminar on the express condition that participants arrived at the training center for a 7 a.m. start.

Q5: How can each participant's line manager be engaged and satisfied?

A: By giving them an active role and a visible payback. The pre-program exercises that form an integral part of the initiative (see Chapter 6) should enable the participant to discuss with the line manager his or her current or future objectives in the context of the topic under consideration (project leadership, time management, teambuilding etc.).

A key contribution of the line manager should be to help the participant "frame" his or her needs from the program, either in the training needs analysis exercise or on the day. This in turn will enable the organizers to tailor group assignments or syndicate work so that the outputs provide each participant with specific solutions to current or prospective challenges back in the workplace.

Q6: What is the essential role of the HR practitioner?

A: The bottom line is that he or she should have a sufficient grasp of the organization's needs to identify the focus of the initiative and negotiate the appropriate resources. HR practitioners are also critical in informing, advising and supervising the work of any suppliers bought in to either design or contribute to specific activities; as well as ensuring that the learning or skills acquired during the initiative have been properly taken on board and sustained.

Depending on the size and resources of the organization, HR practitioners may also be actively involved in the design and delivery of the essential components. But this role is secondary to the ones above. This issue is explored in greater detail in Chapter 6.

Index

action learning 95-8, 130, 132
address list 139-45
appraisals 125-7
Argyris, Professor Chris 129-30
Arthur Andersen 111-15
assignments 43-5, 104
assumptions, testing 77-88, 103-4, 148

behavior patterns 129-30, 131-2
benchmarking 57-9
"blended learning" 42-6, 49
books 134-6
Borges, Antonio 5-6, 8
Bosch 53
BP 23-4
brainstorming 44-5
Buller, Caroline 12

Cable & Wireless MBA for Telecommunications 110
Capstone 46-7
career management 125-7, 156
case studies
    see also examples
    News International 47-8
    Volkswagen/Skoda 62-8

Celmi Experience 95-6
Channel 4 42-3
Charlton, David 95-7
China, cultural barriers 76-7
choosing suppliers 100-103, 148-9
collective insight 125
communication ability 125
competencies 65-7, 74-5, 122-5
Concord School of Management 107
consortia 59-61
consortium programs 115-18, 119
context 9-10, 15
corporate learning centers 14, 109-110
corporate "universities" 14, 106-111, 118
Cranfield School of Management 12
critical success factors 71, 73-4, 122, 131
cross-company alliances 59-61
cultural barriers 76-7

design 88-103
distance learning 27-8, 38-41
diversity 151-2
double loop learning 129-30

e-learning   36-8
  providers   136-9
efmd *see* European Foundation for
  Management Development
electronic brainstorming   44-5
engaging management   157-8
environmental awareness   4
environmental issues   149
Ericsson Management Institute
  108-9
European Foundation for
  Management Development (efmd)
  3-4, 109-110
European Institute of Business
  Administration (INSEAD)   21
examples
  Hong Kong Government
    1992-97 71-5, 93-5
  insurance company   91-2
  international law firm   78-85,
    89-90
  local community primary school
    85-8, 97-8
  University of Oulu   99-100
expatriates   52-62

fast track career schemes   125-6,
  131
Fonda, Nickie   123-4
frequently asked questions (FAQs)
  155-8

General Electric   56-7, 107-8
globalization   51-68
Grand Metropolitan   58
Gratton, Professor Lynda   2, 126-7
group assignments   44-5

"halo" effect   126, 131
Hamel, Gary   123-4
Hammond, Val   27, 127

Hayes, Chris   123-4
Henley Management College   40-41,
  58-9, 110
Hewlett Packard   54
Hirsh, Dr Wendy   10, 29, 76, 124,
  126
Hong Kong   71-5, 77-8, 93-5
HR practitioner role   14, 15, 31-3,
  152-3, 158
human interactions   12-14, 15, 125
human resources approach   71,
  122-3, 131

in-house training   22-4
individual assignments   43-4
individual insight   125
INSEAD *see* European Institute of
  Business Administration
interactions   12-14, 15, 125
International Distillers   54
Internet   28, 35-49, 104, 156
intranets   42-3
"intrepreneurs"   125
intuitive vision   4

Japan, cultural barriers   76

Kakabadse, Professor Andrew   76,
  124-5
Kerr, Steven   32
key aspects
  concepts   121-32
  frequently asked questions (FAQs)
    155-8
  resources   133-45
  ten steps   147-53
  thinkers   121-32
knowledge transfer   57-9

language systems   10-11, 124, 148
lateral thinking   4

learning needs approach   71, 123, 131
learning objectives   149-50
London Business School   59-60
Lorange, Peter   102

M&S *see* Marks & Spencer
management education   18-22, 34
management training   18, 22-4
management vocabularies   10-11, 124, 148
Marks & Spencer (M&S)   2-3, 117-18
MBA programs   12-14, 20-22, 29-31, 40-41, 110-115
measurements   155
mental models   128
metaphorical analogies   4
Mintzberg, Henry   8
Moore, Mark   8-9, 10
Moss Kanter, Professor Rosabeth   125-6
Mount Everest   96

NatWest Education and Learning Centre   109-110
needs analysis   77-8, 86-90, 97-8, 122-5, 148
News International, case study   47-8

ONA *see* organizational needs analysis
"organizational competence"   28-9
organizational learning   127-30
organizational needs analysis (ONA)   77-8, 86-8
outdoor learning   95-8

personal mastery   128
plenary discussion   98-100, 104
Prahalad, C.K.   123-4
preparation   88-90, 104
presentation   90-92
"princes"   126, 131

research   12-14, 43-4
resources   133-45
results capture   150-51
Revans, Reg   130
Roffey Park Management Institute   5
Roos, Professor Johan   11

Salama, Eric   40, 41-2, 46
scenarios   70, 92-5, 104, 122, 131
"scientific management"   19
Senge, Peter   127-8
shapers   13
shared visions   128
simulations   92-5
Sinetar, Marsha   125
Skoda, case study   62-8
snakes and ladders exercise   43
sounding boards   13
sponsors   13
Standard Chartered Bank   40-41, 58-9, 60-61
Star Alliance   59
Stopford, John   128-9
strategic alliances   59-61
strategic competence assessment   71, 123, 131
strategy   4-5, 70-75, 103
sustained learning   151
syndicate discussion   98-100, 104
syndicate work   150-51
systems thinking   127-9

tailored degrees   111-15, 118-19
tailored development   11-12, 15
Taylor, Frederick Winslow   19
team learning   128
testing assumptions   77-88, 103-4, 148
thinkers   121-32
timelines   32-3, 37

training needs analysis (TNA) 11,
    77-8, 80-85, 89-90, 97-8, 128
Tungsram 56-7

United States (US), capital expansion
    19

Velvet Revolution 52
videoconferencing 45
Volkswagen, case study 62-8

websites 136-9
work-life agenda 127